The *All-American* OUTDOOR

COOKBOOK

President: Thomas F. McDow III
Vice President: Dave Kempf
Managing Editor: Mary Cummings
Project Editor: Ginger Dawson
Contributing Editor: Nicki Pendleton Wood
Creative and Product Manager: Kristy McIntosh
Project Coordinator: Mary Wilson
Art Director: Steve Newman
Typographers: Jessie Anglin, Sara Anglin
Essayist: Laura Hill
Production Manager: Mark Sloan
Manufacturing Coordinator: Powell Ropp

Cover and Book Design: Jim Scott

The All-American Outdoor Cookbook is a collection of our favorite
recipes, which are not necessarily original recipes.

Published by Favorite Recipes® Press
an imprint of

FRP

2451 Atrium Way
Nashville, Tennessee 37214

Copyright 2000 by
Great American Opportunities Inc.
ISBN: 0-87197-832-6

Manufactured in
the United States of America
Copies: 30,000

Contents

Great American Outdoors 4

1 Portable Feasts 7

2 Campfire Cooking 27

3 Great Grilling 55

4 Outdoor Celebrations 91

5 Outdoor Essentials 115

Index 121

Great American Outdoors

Since first discovering what fire could do for food, mankind has enjoyed outdoor cooking, savoring the delights of great food served amidst the beauty of nature. Outdoor cooking is found in all cultures, of course. But perhaps no people have made it so much their own as Americans.

Early settlers were using the word barbecue (from a Haitian word for the wooden framework meat was cooked on) as early as 1709 in America. By the 1730s, a barbecue had come to mean a social gathering. In 1850, one Kansas barbecue boasted food that included six cattle and a hundred hams, in addition to literally tons of other meat and baked dishes.

Since the caveman days, we've refined our tastes, to be sure, rejecting grilled mastodon in favor of juicy hamburgers or saucy chicken. But the basic appeal of outdoor cooking remains timeless. Today, Americans light up more than 1.8 billion outdoor cooking fires each year, not to mention the rapidly increasing popularity of gas and electric grilling in these healthful and environmentally conscious times.

One of the attractions of outdoor cuisine is that it is relaxed and casual. Dressy clothes are hanging in the closet, and we're happily decked out in sneakers and shorts. We haven't spent the day polishing furniture for a big-deal dinner. And we won't have to spend half the night putting away the good silver and china afterwards. Whether we're laying out a sumptuous spread for a pre-game tailgate party or whipping up S'Mores for a troop of Girl Scouts on a hike, when we cook out we're cooking easy.

Nearly everyone enjoys cooking outside (not to mention eating the end results), and even those with only basic indoor cooking skills can learn how to prepare great food out of doors.

In this book, you will find that outdoor cooking is just as full of variety and creativity as indoor cuisine. In fact, nearly anything that can be prepared in a kitchen can be adapted successfully to outdoor cooking, right down to delicious hors d'oeuvre and tempting baked goods and desserts.

In **Portable Feasts** we have collected a number of wonderful ideas for your next picnic or tailgate party. We have also found lots of recipes for **Campfire Cooking**, including great new ways with traditional campfire fare and fresh new ideas you will want to try next time you camp out.

The pages devoted to **Great Grilling** will expand your current repertoire and offer tips on perfecting your grilling technique. Finally, we have gone all-out on **Outdoor Celebrations**, such a big part of our relaxed social and family lives.

As an extra help to our readers, we have also included a section at the back of the book, **Outdoor Essentials**, with charts, diagrams, and ideas to help you get the most from cooking in the great American outdoors.

"Summer cooking implies
a sense of immediacy, a capacity to capture
the essence of the fleeting moment."
— Elizabeth David

"To barbecue is a way of life rather than a desirable method of cooking."
— Clement Freud

"I'm a man. Men cook outside . . . .That outdoor grilling is a manly pursuit has long been beyond question. If this wasn't understood, you'd never get grown men to put on those aprons with pictures of dancing wienies and things on the front, and messages like 'Come N' Get It.' . . . Try putting that stuff on the family dog."
— William Geist

Some 83 percent of U.S. households own a barbecue grill.

Portable Feasts

If your childhood memories of picnics are clouded with visions of anemic potato salad and soggy fried chicken, get your picnic blanket out and dust off the hamper. We're about to change your mind forever about eating out in the great outdoors.

Today, picnics are creative, delicious events that can be put together at a moment's notice or prepared far ahead for convenience. No longer are we limited to the traditional weekend sandwich lunch, either; today's picnics are just as likely to include breakfast or dinner.

In **Portable Feasts,** you'll find everything from elegant menus for the sophisticated cook to easy-to-make, easy-to-eat snacks for kids. Even special events like a summer evening concert present a great opportunity for an outdoor feast.

For a change, try a theme picnic. Our *Road Rally Picnic* menu gives old favorites a good-natured automotive flair. Inveterate tailgaters will cheer winning menus that lend themselves beautifully to parking lot festivities.

Without a car? We've got you covered in our *Banquet on Wheels,* an Italian-flavored feast that fits nicely in a bicycle basket—or a back pack. And remember, even if it rains there's no excuse for not having a picnic; all of these menus will taste almost as good indoors as they do under the trees.

BANQUET ON WHEELS

Slim Jim Breadsticks

Dill Dip

Asparagus, Broccoli and Cauliflower Dippers

Seafood Pasta Salad

Cold Broiled Chicken

Stromboli Bread

Pecan Oatmeal Chewies

Yummy Bars

Peddle (or drive) to the perfect shade tree to enjoy this portable Italian feast. Package everything in sealable plastic bags to spread on a blanket once you've found your spot. Carry along bottled water for an easy thirst quencher.

SLIM JIM BREADSTICKS

8 unsplit frankfurter rolls
½ cup butter, softened
¼ cup Parmesan cheese

Cut rolls into quarters lengthwise. Spread all sides with butter. Roll breadsticks in Parmesan cheese. Place on ungreased baking sheet. Bake at 250 degrees until crisp. May roll breadsticks in minced parsley, finely chopped nuts and/or poppy seed.

Yield: 32 breadsticks

DILL DIP

1 cup sour cream
⅔ cup mayonnaise
1 tablespoon parsley flakes
1 teaspoon grated onion
1 teaspoon dillseed
1 teaspoon seasoned salt

Combine sour cream, mayonnaise, parsley flakes, onion, dillseed and seasoned salt in bowl; mix well. Chill, covered, in refrigerator for 14 hours or longer. Serve with breadsticks and bite-size fresh vegetables such as asparagus, broccoli and cauliflower.

Yield: 6 servings

SEAFOOD PASTA SALAD

8 ounces rainbow corkscrew pasta
1 cup broccoli flowerets
½ cup low-fat mayonnaise
¼ bottle of Italian salad dressing
¼ cup Parmesan cheese
8 ounces chopped imitation crab meat
½ cup sliced black olives
½ cup chopped green bell pepper
½ cup chopped tomato
¼ cup sliced green onions
1 tablespoon parsley flakes
1 teaspoon oregano
½ teaspoon dill
½ teaspoon celery salt

Cook pasta using package directions. Rinse in cold water; drain. Cook broccoli in a small amount of water in saucepan until tender-crisp; drain. Combine mayonnaise, salad dressing and Parmesan cheese in large bowl; mix well. Add pasta, broccoli, crab meat, black olives, green pepper, tomato, green onions and seasonings; toss lightly. Chill until serving time.

Yield: 6 servings

COLD BROILED CHICKEN

½ cup soy sauce
1 cup orange juice
1 tablespoon paprika
2 cloves of garlic, minced
Dash of hot pepper sauce
6 chicken breasts, split
½ cup corn oil

Combine soy sauce, orange juice, paprika, garlic and hot pepper sauce in bowl. Add chicken. Marinate, covered, for 1 to 2 hours, turning occasionally. Remove chicken from marinade. Brush with oil. Place bone side up on rack in broiler pan. Broil for 13 minutes. Baste with marinade. Broil for 3 minutes longer. Turn chicken; move a little further from heat source to avoid blistering. Baste skin side with marinade. Broil for 12 minutes. Baste again. Broil until tender. Let stand until cool. Wrap in foil. Chill until serving time.

Yield: 6 servings

STROMBOLI BREAD

1 (16-ounce) package frozen bread dough, thawed
12 ounces pepperoni, finely chopped
5 hard-boiled eggs, finely chopped
4 cups shredded sharp Cheddar cheese
2 cups shredded mozzarella cheese
2 tablespoons milk

Divide bread dough into 2 portions. Roll 1 portion into rectangle on greased baking sheet. Combine pepperoni, eggs and Cheddar cheese in bowl; mix well. Spread over dough. Sprinkle with mozzarella cheese. Roll remaining dough into rectangle; place over cheese. Brush top with milk. Bake at 350 degrees for 20 to 25 minutes or until golden brown. Cut into squares.

Yield: 6 servings

PECAN OATMEAL CHEWIES

½ cup margarine
½ cup packed brown sugar
⅓ cup honey
¼ teaspoon cinnamon
2 cups old-fashioned oats
1 cup chopped dates
⅓ cup coarsely chopped pecans
¼ cup raisins

Combine margarine, brown sugar and honey in saucepan. Bring to a boil over medium-high heat, stirring constantly; reduce heat. Simmer for 4 minutes; remove from heat. Stir in cinnamon, oats, dates, pecans and raisins. Chill for 1 hour. Shape into 1-inch balls; place on plate. Chill until firm. Store in airtight container in refrigerator.

Yield: 3 dozen

YUMMY BARS

1 (2-layer) package German chocolate cake mix
¾ cup melted butter
⅓ cup evaporated milk
1 cup chocolate chips
1 cup chopped nuts
50 caramels
⅓ cup evaporated milk

Combine cake mix, butter and ⅓ cup evaporated milk in bowl; mix well. Pat half the mixture into 9×13-inch baking pan. Bake at 350 degrees for 6 to 8 minutes. Sprinkle with chocolate chips and nuts. Melt caramels in glass bowl in microwave, stirring frequently. Blend in ⅓ cup evaporated milk. Pour over chocolate chips and nuts. Spoon remaining cake mix mixture over top. Bake for 15 to 20 minutes longer. Cool. Cut into bars.

Yield: 32 bars

PICNIC IN A PAIL

Knots on a Log

Apple Snackers   Bananawiches

Treasure Pops   Goody Cones

Peppermint-Orange Sipper or
Grape Juice Fizzy

Pack lunch in a pail for tiny picnickers. Tuck your choice of our goodies plus a surprise under colorful party napkins. Tie helium-filled balloons to each, and you're off to the park. Add games, a clown, and plenty of fun!

KNOTS ON A LOG

2 celery stalks
2 tablespoons pimento cheese
18 raisins

Cut celery into thirds crosswise. Fill with pimento cheese. Arrange raisins on top. Wrap in colored plastic wrap. Chill until serving time.

Yield: 6 servings

APPLE SNACKERS

6 large apples, cored
6 tablespoons peanut butter or pimento cheese

Wash apples; pat dry. Pack center of each apple with 1 tablespoon peanut butter. Wrap tightly in plastic wrap. Chill for 30 minutes or until filling is set. Cut crosswise into ½-inch slices. Rewrap apples tightly. Chill until serving time.

Yield: 6 servings

BANANAWICHES

12 tablespoons peanut butter
6 hot dog buns, split
6 bananas
6 tablespoons strawberry preserves

Spread 2 tablespoons peanut butter in each hot dog bun. Place 1 banana inside each bun. Spread 1 tablespoon preserves over each banana. Wrap in colored plastic wrap.

Yield: 6 servings

TREASURE POPS

½ cup sugar
½ cup packed light brown sugar
½ cup margarine, softened
1 egg, beaten
½ cup peanut butter
1 teaspoon vanilla extract
1½ cups flour
½ teaspoon baking powder
½ teaspoon baking soda
¼ teaspoon salt
10 wooden sticks
10 fun-size Milky Way candy bars

Combine sugar, brown sugar, margarine, egg, peanut butter and vanilla in bowl; mix well. Add flour, baking powder, baking soda and salt; mix well. Insert wooden stick into each candy bar to form lollipop. Shape about ⅓ cup dough evenly around each candy bar, covering completely. Place 4 inches apart on ungreased baking sheet. Bake at 375 degrees for 13 minutes or until golden brown. Cool on baking sheet for 10 minutes. Remove to wire rack to cool completely. Wrap individually with colored plastic wrap; secure with ribbon or tie.

Yield: 10 cookies

GOODY CONES

¼ cup "M & M's" Chocolate Candies
¼ cup Skittles
¼ cup chocolate chips
¼ cup miniature marshmallows
¼ cup Golden Grahams cereal
¼ cup oyster crackers
¼ cup miniature pretzels
¼ cup shoestring potatoes
¼ cup sunflower seed
¼ cup raisins
¼ cup dates
¼ cup peanuts
6 ice cream cones

Combine chocolate candies, Skittles, chocolate chips, marshmallows, cereal, oyster crackers, pretzels, shoestring potatoes, sunflower seed, raisins, dates and peanuts in bowl; mix well. Spoon into ice cream cones. Wrap in colored plastic wrap.

Yield: 6 cones

PEPPERMINT-ORANGE SIPPER

6 oranges
6 peppermint sticks

Roll each orange between hand and hard surface to make it juicy. Cut small opening in each orange. Insert 1 peppermint stick into each orange. Drink orange by sucking through peppermint stick straw.

Yield: 6 servings

GRAPE JUICE FIZZY

1 quart grape juice, chilled
1 quart lemon-lime soda, chilled

Combine grape juice and soda in chilled thermos jug. Pour into small cartoon paper cups to serve.

Yield: 6 servings

ROAD RALLY PICNIC

Pigs in Mufflers

Pizza Cheese Wheels

Speedy Chicken Wings

Studeabaked Sub

Tail Light Tomatoes

Stuck-in-the-Mud Cake

It's-a-Lemon Bars

Root Beer or Soda Pop on the Rocks

Mark your maps and rally with good friends and great food to an inviting picnic spot. Include the menu on the invitations, and add your own creative ideas.

PIGS IN MUFFLERS

8 sausage links
1 (8-count) can crescent rolls
8 teaspoons Dijon mustard
8 teaspoons shredded Cheddar cheese

Brown sausage in skillet; drain. Unroll dough; separate into triangles. Spread 1 teaspoon mustard on each triangle. Place 1 sausage link and 1 teaspoon cheese over triangle. Roll to enclose sausage and cheese. Place on baking sheet. Bake using package directions.

Yield: 8 servings

PIZZA CHEESE WHEELS

1 pound sharp Cheddar cheese, shredded
1 onion, chopped
1 (4-ounce) can chopped black olives
1 green bell pepper, chopped
1 (4-ounce) jar pimentos, drained
1 (6-ounce) can tomato paste
½ cup vegetable oil
6 onion-flavored bagels, split
Salt and pepper to taste
Oregano and garlic powder to taste

Combine cheese, onion, black olives, green pepper, pimentos, tomato paste and oil in bowl; mix well. Spoon onto bagels. Sprinkle with salt, pepper, oregano and garlic powder. Place on baking sheet. Bake for 15 minutes.

Yield: 12 servings

SPEEDY CHICKEN WINGS

½ cup margarine
1 cup Texas Pete sauce
2 tablespoons brown sugar
2 tablespoons Worcestershire sauce
1 (24-count) package chicken wings
Vegetable oil for deep-frying

Melt margarine in small saucepan. Stir in Texas Pete sauce, brown sugar and Worcestershire sauce. Deep-fry chicken wings in hot oil in deep-fryer until wings float to top and are golden brown. Place wings in casserole. Add sauce. Cover casserole. Shake until wings are covered with sauce.

Yield: 8 servings

STUDEABAKED SUB

1 loaf frozen bread dough
4 ounces roast beef, sliced
4 ounces cooked ham, sliced
8 ounces Swiss cheese, sliced
1 (4-ounce) can mushroom pieces, drained

Thaw bread and let rise using package directions. Roll into ⅛-inch thick rectangle on floured surface. Alternate layers of roast beef, ham, cheese and mushrooms down center. Fold in sides to enclose filling. Seal edge; tuck ends under. Place in 9×13-inch baking pan. Bake using package directions for bread.

Yield: 6 servings

TAIL LIGHT TOMATOES

6 tomatoes, peeled, sliced
1 onion, sliced
2½ tablespoons vegetable oil
1 tablespoon lemon juice
1 clove of garlic, minced
1 teaspoon tarragon
1 teaspoon basil
1 teaspoon dried parsley
1 teaspoon salt
¼ teaspoon pepper

Place tomatoes and onion in shallow dish. Combine oil, lemon juice, garlic, tarragon, basil, parsley, salt and pepper in small bowl; mix well. Pour over vegetables. Let stand at room temperature for 15 minutes.

Yield: 6 servings

STUCK-IN-THE-MUD CAKE

1 cup margarine
½ cup baking cocoa
2 cups sugar
4 eggs
1½ cups flour
⅛ teaspoon salt
1 cup chopped pecans
1 cup miniature marshmallows
5 tablespoons melted margarine
½ cup (or less) baking cocoa
½ cup milk
1 (1-pound) package confectioners' sugar

Melt 1 cup margarine with ½ cup cocoa in saucepan. Remove from heat; blend well. Add sugar and eggs; mix well. Mix in flour, salt and pecans. Spoon into greased and floured 9×13-inch cake pan. Bake at 350 degrees for 30 to 40 minutes or until cake tests done. Sprinkle marshmallows over top. Blend melted margarine and ½ cup cocoa in mixer bowl. Mix in remaining ingredients. Spread over top. Let stand until cool.

Yield: 12 servings

IT'S-A-LEMON BARS

1 cup butter, softened
2 cups flour
½ cup confectioners' sugar
2 cups sugar
¼ cup flour
1 teaspoon baking powder
4 eggs, beaten
6 tablespoons lemon juice

Mix first 3 ingredients in bowl until crumbly. Pat into 9×13-inch baking pan. Bake at 350 degrees for 15 minutes or until light brown. Spread mixture of sugar, ¼ cup flour, baking powder, eggs and lemon juice over baked layer. Bake for 25 to 30 minutes or until light brown. Cool. Sprinkle with confectioners' sugar. Cut into bars.

Yield: 2 dozen

STEEPLECHASE PICNIC

Cucumber-Onion Salad

Spinach Dip in Bread Bowl

Cornish Pastries or Assorted Finger Sandwiches

Stuffed Mushrooms

Glorified Shortbread

Fresh Strawberries   **Spot of Tea**

Pack a classic wicker hamper with English treats, and spend the day watching the races or the river flowing by. Or serve this picnic on a blanket at home while watching tennis at Wimbledon or the Irish Derby. Use real china, glasses, and silverware, and celebrate your favorite sport.

CUCUMBER-ONION SALAD

5 cucumbers, peeled, sliced
2 cups water
1 tablespoon salt
1 onion, sliced, separated into rings
½ cup sugar
½ cup vinegar
¼ teaspoon chopped fresh parsley
½ teaspoon salt
⅛ teaspoon pepper

Combine cucumber slices, water and 1 tablespoon salt in bowl. Let stand for 1 hour; drain. Add onion rings; set aside. Combine sugar, vinegar, parsley, ½ teaspoon salt and pepper in jar; mix well. Pour over vegetables; toss gently. Chill, covered, for 30 minutes.

Yield: 4 servings

SPINACH DIP IN BREAD BOWL

1 round loaf sourdough bread
1/3 cup melted margarine
2/3 cup chopped green bell pepper
1/3 cup each chopped celery and onion
1 pound Velveeta cheese, cut up
1 (10-ounce) package frozen chopped spinach,
    thawed, squeezed dry
1/4 teaspoon dried rosemary leaves

Cut top from loaf; scoop out and reserve center, leaving 1-inch shell. Cut reserved bread into bite-size pieces. Brush inside of shell with margarine; place loaf on baking sheet. Bake at 350 degrees for 20 minutes. Sauté green pepper, celery and onion in remaining margarine in skillet until tender. Add cheese. Cook over low heat until cheese melts, stirring constantly. Stir spinach and rosemary into cheese mixture. Spoon into bread shell. Serve with bread pieces.

Yield: 2⅔ cups

CORNISH PASTRIES

4 (12-ounce) short crust pastries
12 ounces lean steak, chopped
4 ounces potato, finely chopped
1 onion, finely chopped
Salt and pepper to taste
1 carrot, finely chopped
1 turnip, finely chopped
2 teaspoons margarine

Roll pastry into four 8-inch rounds on floured surface. Combine steak, potato, onion, salt, pepper, carrot and turnip in bowl; mix well. Add 1/4 of mixture to each pastry. Dampen edge of pastry with water; fold to form half a circle. Press edges to seal; cut vent. Place 1/2 teaspoon margarine in each vent. Place in 8-inch round baking pans. Bake at 400 degrees for 20 minutes. Reduce temperature to 350 degrees. Bake on middle rack for 40 minutes longer.

Yield: 4 servings

STUFFED MUSHROOMS

36 medium mushrooms
16 ounces low-fat cream cheese, softened
1 to 2 (7-ounce) cans crab meat
Garlic powder to taste
1/2 teaspoon lemon juice
3/4 to 1 cup shredded Cheddar cheese

Wash mushrooms; discard stems. Place mushroom caps on baking sheet. Mix cream cheese, crab meat, garlic powder and lemon juice in bowl. Fill mushroom caps; sprinkle with Cheddar cheese. Bake until cheese melts. Chill until serving time.

Yield: 4 servings

GLORIFIED SHORTBREAD

2 cups flour
1/2 cup confectioners' sugar
1 1/2 teaspoons cornstarch
1 cup butter
2 eggs, beaten
1 cup sugar
1 cup walnuts
1 cup coconut
1 tablespoon flour
1/8 teaspoon baking powder

Combine 2 cups flour, confectioners' sugar and cornstarch in bowl. Cut in butter until crumbly. Press into 9×13-inch baking pan. Bake at 350 degrees for 15 minutes. Combine eggs, sugar, walnuts, coconut, 1 tablespoon flour and baking powder in bowl; mix well. Spoon onto top of partially cooked shortbread. Bake for 15 minutes longer. Cool completely. Cut into bars.

Yield: 2 dozen

PICNIC IN THE PARK

Pickled Mushrooms

Yummy Fruit Dip

Assorted Fresh Fruit

Parsley-Bulgur Salad

Pita Twins

Carrot-Walnut Cake

Iced Coffee

Picnic at a concert in the park with a foreign flair. Pita pockets make perfect take-alongs—just pack the spicy fillings separately. Add purchased olives, assorted cheeses and baklava for a balmy midsummer's night spread.

PICKLED MUSHROOMS

⅓ cup red wine vinegar
⅓ cup vegetable oil
1 tablespoon brown sugar
1 small onion, thinly sliced
1 teaspoon prepared mustard
2 tablespoons parsley flakes
1 teaspoon salt
3 (8-ounce) cans button mushrooms, drained

Combine vinegar, oil, brown sugar, onion, mustard, parsley flakes and salt in saucepan; mix well. Bring to a boil. Add mushrooms. Cook for 5 to 10 minutes or to desired consistency. Cool completely. Marinate in refrigerator for 24 hours or longer.

Yield: 6 servings

YUMMY FRUIT DIP

¼ cup sugar
8 ounces cream cheese, softened
¾ cup packed brown sugar
1 teaspoon vanilla extract
Milk

Combine sugar, cream cheese, brown sugar and vanilla in mixer bowl; mix well. Add enough milk to make of desired consistency. Chill in airtight container. Serve with bite-size fresh fruit.

Yield: 6 to 8 servings

PARSLEY-BULGUR SALAD

½ cup bulgur
1½ cups finely chopped parsley
½ cup finely chopped fresh mint
3 green onions, finely chopped
1 large tomato, chopped
6 tablespoons lemon juice
¼ cup olive oil
Salt to taste
1 head romaine lettuce

Rinse bulgur in water; drain and squeeze dry. Combine bulgur, parsley, mint, green onions and tomato in bowl; mix well. Add lemon juice, olive oil and salt; mix well. Line salad bowl with lettuce leaves. Spoon mixture into bowl. Use lettuce leaves as edible spoons to scoop out salad.

Yield: 6 servings

OUTDOOR LORE

Take along "fun packs" or covered cake pans filled with games, books, toys, and coloring materials for in-car fun. Children can color or play on the closed top.

Turkey Sausage Filling

1 pound turkey sausage
2 tablespoons lemon juice
Pinch of cinnamon
Pinch of nutmeg
1 clove of garlic, minced
2 tablespoons chopped mint
½ teaspoon oregano
1 tablespoon chopped parsley
1 onion, thinly sliced
1 tomato, chopped
½ cup sliced deli-style pickles

Shape turkey sausage into tiny meatballs. Brown meatballs in large skillet sprayed with nonstick cooking spray; drain. Add lemon juice, seasonings, onion, tomato and pickle slices. Simmer, covered, for 2 to 3 minutes or just until vegetables are tender-crisp.

Fruity Burger Filling

½ cup chopped onion
½ cup chopped celery
1 tablespoon vegetable oil
1 pound ground beef
1 medium red Delicious apple, chopped
¼ cup dark raisins
1 teaspoon curry powder

Sauté onion and celery in oil in skillet. Add ground beef. Cook until crumbly, stirring constantly; drain. Stir in apple, raisins and curry powder. Simmer for several minutes or just until apple is tender-crisp.

Pita Twins

6 small pita rounds, cut into halves
Turkey Sausage Filling
Fruity Burger Filling
2 cups plain yogurt

Fill half the pita pockets with Turkey Sausage Filling. Spoon Fruity Burger Filling into remaining pita pockets. Top each with yogurt.

Yield: 6 servings

Carrot-Walnut Cake

Shortening
1¼ cups flour
1 cup sugar
1½ teaspoons baking powder
1 teaspoon salt
2 teaspoons cinnamon
¾ cup vegetable oil
2 eggs
2 teaspoons vanilla extract
1 cup grated carrots
1 cup walnuts, chopped
½ cup raisins
2 cups confectioners' sugar, sifted
2 tablespoons margarine, softened
Milk

Grease bottom of 8×8-inch cake pan with a small amount of shortening. Combine flour, sugar, baking powder, salt, cinnamon, oil, eggs and vanilla in large mixer bowl. Beat for 1 minute at low speed or until blended. Beat for 2 minutes at medium speed. Stir in carrots, walnuts and raisins. Pour into prepared cake pan. Bake at 325 degrees for 40 to 45 minutes or until wooden pick inserted in center comes out clean. Let stand until cool. Cream confectioners' sugar and margarine in mixer bowl. Add 1 tablespoon milk at a time, mixing well after each addition until of spreading consistency. Spread frosting over cooled cake. Sprinkle with additional walnuts.

Yield: 6 servings

TAILGATE BRUNCH

Sausage Balls

Easy Fruit Salad

Scrambled Egg Casserole

Garlic Cheese Grits

Slow-Cooker Apples

**Peabody Muffins or
Lemon Raspberry Muffins**

Assorted Juices

Hot Coffee

Brunch is a great way to tailgate before an early game and easy if the menu is make-ahead like this one. Keep tailgating equipment—dishes, utensils, folding table and chairs—ready to go and have everyone bring a dish to make weekly parties extra simple.

SAUSAGE BALLS

1 pound Cheddar cheese, shredded
1 pound hot pork sausage
3 cups baking mix

Combine cheese, sausage and baking mix in bowl; mix well. Roll into small balls. Place on baking sheet. Bake at 350 degrees for 20 minutes or until brown.

Yield: 4 dozen

EASY FRUIT SALAD

1 (15-ounce) can pineapple chunks
1 (4-ounce) package instant French vanilla pudding
1 (16-ounce) can chunky mixed fruit, drained
1 cup seedless white grapes, cut into halves
2 cups miniature marshmallows
4 small bananas, sliced

Drain pineapple, reserving juice. Combine pineapple juice and pudding mix in bowl; mix well. Combine pineapple, mixed fruit, grapes and marshmallows in bowl. Stir in pudding. Chill, covered, for 1 hour or until serving time. Add bananas just before serving.

Yield: 8 to 10 servings

SCRAMBLED EGG CASSEROLE

3 tablespoons flour
2 tablespoons butter
2 cups milk
1/4 cup chopped green onions
3 tablespoons butter
1 cup shredded Cheddar cheese
1 pound bacon, crisp-fried, crumbled
12 eggs, scrambled
1 (4-ounce) jar button mushrooms
Salt and pepper to taste
1/2 cup buttered bread crumbs
1/2 teaspoon paprika

Combine flour and 2 tablespoons butter in saucepan. Stir in milk. Cook until thickened, stirring constantly. Sauté green onions in 3 tablespoons butter in skillet. Stir green onions into milk mixture. Add cheese. Stir until melted. Add bacon, eggs, mushrooms, salt and pepper; mix well. Pour into buttered 9×12-inch casserole. Top with bread crumbs; sprinkle with paprika. Chill overnight. Bake at 350 degrees for 30 minutes.

Yield: 8 to 10 servings

GARLIC CHEESE GRITS

1 egg
¼ cup (about) milk
4 cups water
1 cup uncooked grits
1 teaspoon salt
½ cup margarine
5 ounces garlic cheese
1 teaspoon Worcestershire sauce
Dash of Tabasco sauce
1 cup shredded sharp Cheddar cheese

Break egg into glass measure. Add enough milk to measure ½ cup. Bring water to a boil in saucepan. Stir in grits and salt. Cook for 5 minutes or until thickened, stirring constantly. Stir in margarine and garlic cheese until melted. Add milk mixture, Worcestershire sauce and Tabasco sauce; mix well. Spoon into greased 9×13-inch baking dish. Bake at 350 degrees for 40 minutes. Top with Cheddar cheese. Let stand until cheese melts.

Yield: 8 to 10 servings

SLOW-COOKER APPLES

6 to 8 apples
½ cup raisins
1 cup chopped pecans
1 cup packed brown sugar
1 teaspoon cinnamon
½ teaspoon nutmeg
2 tablespoons butter
½ cup water

Peel top ⅓ of apples; remove core. Combine raisins, pecans and brown sugar in bowl; mix well. Spoon into apple cavities. Place in slow cooker. Sprinkle with cinnamon and nutmeg; dot with butter. Add water. Cook on Low for 8 hours to overnight.

Yield: 6 to 8 servings

PEABODY MUFFINS

4 cups sifted flour
2 cups sugar
1 tablespoon baking powder
½ teaspoon salt
½ cup butter, melted
2 cups milk
2 eggs
1 tablespoon vanilla extract

Sift flour, sugar, baking powder and salt together into large mixer bowl. Make well in center. Add mixture of butter, milk, eggs and vanilla. Stir with fork just until moistened. Fill greased muffin cups ⅔ full. Bake at 400 degrees for 20 to 25 minutes.

Yield: 2 dozen

LEMON RASPBERRY MUFFINS

2 cups sifted flour
1 cup sugar
1 tablespoon baking powder
½ teaspoon salt
1 cup half-and-half
½ cup vegetable oil
1 teaspoon lemon extract
2 eggs
1 cup frozen raspberries, thawed, drained

Combine flour, sugar, baking powder and salt in large bowl; mix well. Blend half-and-half, oil, lemon extract and eggs in small bowl. Add to flour mixture. Stir just until moistened. Fold in raspberries gently. Fill paper-lined muffin cups ¾ full. Bake at 425 degrees for 18 to 23 minutes or until golden brown. Cool for 5 minutes. Remove to wire rack to cool completely.

Yield: 1 dozen

Citrus Bowl Tailgate

Romaine-Tangerine Salad

Fruit Kabobs with Citrus Dip

Oriental Chicken Pitas or Orange Jubilee Chicken

Sweet-Sour Lamb Skewers

Chocolate Chip Muffins

Victory Dessert Pizza

Four-Fruit Punch

Tailgating captures the essence of team spirit and good eating whether at the stadium parking lot or in front of the television set. Just pick your favorite team of food specialties and enjoy!

Romaine-Tangerine Salad

1 bunch romaine lettuce
6 green onions, sliced
Segments of 4 tangerines
⅓ cup vegetable oil
3 tablespoons sugar
3 tablespoons vinegar
⅛ teaspoon pepper
½ cup sliced almonds
2 tablespoons sugar
2 teaspoons water

Combine lettuce, green onions and tangerines in large zip-lock plastic bag; seal. Chill in refrigerator. Combine oil, 3 tablespoons sugar, vinegar and pepper in jar. Cover; shake vigorously. Chill in refrigerator. Combine almonds, remaining 2 tablespoons sugar and water in glass bowl.

Microwave for 3 to 4 minutes, stirring several times. Add dressing to lettuce mixture in plastic bag; shake to coat. Place in salad bowl. Add almonds; toss to mix.

Yield: 8 servings

Fruit Kabobs

1 cantaloupe, cut into chunks
½ honeydew melon, cut into chunks
1 pint strawberries, hulls removed
Segments of 2 oranges
2 bananas, cut into chunks
2 apples, sliced
2 tablespoons lemon juice

Brush fruit with lemon juice. Thread onto skewers. Arrange skewers spoke-fashion on tray. Spoon Citrus Dip into bowl in center.

Yield: 24 servings

Citrus Dip

1 tablespoon flour
⅓ cup sugar
1 egg, beaten
½ cup pineapple juice
⅓ cup strained fresh orange juice
¼ cup strained fresh lemon juice
½ cup whipping cream, whipped

Combine flour and sugar in small saucepan; mix well. Stir in egg and fruit juices. Cook over medium heat for 5 minutes or until thickened, stirring constantly. Chill for 10 minutes. Fold in whipped cream gently. Chill until serving time.

Yield: 2 cups

ORIENTAL CHICKEN PITAS

4 cups chopped cooked chicken
2 cups grapefruit segments
1 cup orange segments
1 cup chopped celery
1 cup chopped green bell pepper
½ cup chopped onion
½ cup halved seedless green grapes
¼ cup sliced green olives
1 cup mayonnaise
¼ cup prepared mustard
1 tablespoon grated orange rind
1 teaspoon ground ginger
½ teaspoon salt
¼ teaspoon pepper
3 (6-count) packages large pita bread

Combine chicken, grapefruit, orange, celery, green pepper, onion, grapes and olives in large bowl. Combine mayonnaise, prepared mustard, orange rind, ginger, salt and pepper in small bowl; mix well. Pour over chicken mixture; toss to coat. Chill in refrigerator. Cut pita bread into halves; open to form pocket. Spoon ½ cup filling into each pocket.

Yield: 10 to 12 servings

ORANGE JUBILEE CHICKEN

1½ cups water
2 cups chopped celery
7 cups fresh whole wheat bread crumbs
1 teaspoon salt
1 cup butter
⅓ cup chopped onion
4 chicken breasts, boned, skinned and split
⅔ cup sugar
3 tablespoons flour
2 eggs, beaten
2 cups orange juice
½ cup chicken broth

Bring water to a boil in medium saucepan. Add celery; reduce heat. Simmer for 5 minutes. Drain, reserving ⅔ cup liquid. Combine bread crumbs, celery, reserved liquid and salt in large bowl. Melt butter in small skillet. Add onion. Sauté until tender. Add to bread mixture; mix well. Form 8 mounds of bread mixture in large shallow baking pan. Place 1 uncooked chicken breast on each mound. Combine sugar, flour, eggs, orange juice and broth in top of double boiler. Cook until thickened, stirring constantly. Spoon half the sauce over chicken. Bake at 350 degrees for 40 minutes or until chicken is tender. Serve with remaining sauce.

Yield: 8 servings

SWEET-SOUR LAMB SKEWERS

2 pounds boneless lamb shoulder or leg
¾ cup orange juice
¼ cup vegetable oil
⅓ cup chopped onion
1½ teaspoons salt
1 teaspoon grated orange rind
1 teaspoon oregano
½ teaspoon marjoram
1 clove of garlic, minced
3 medium green bell peppers, cut into chunks
24 mushroom caps
24 cherry tomatoes
2 oranges, cut into 8 wedges, cut into halves
1 (16-ounce) can pineapple chunks, drained

Trim lamb; cut into 1½ to 2-inch cubes. Place in large bowl. Combine next 8 ingredients in bowl; pour over lamb. Chill, covered, for several hours to overnight. Remove lamb from marinade; reserve marinade. Arrange lamb, green peppers, mushrooms, tomatoes, orange wedges and pineapple chunks on skewers. Brush with marinade. Broil 6 to 8 inches from heat source for 18 to 20 minutes or until done to taste, turning and brushing with marinade several times.

Yield: 6 to 8 servings

CHOCOLATE CHIP MUFFINS

4 cups flour
2/3 cup sugar
2/3 cup packed brown sugar
4 teaspoons baking powder
1 teaspoon baking soda
1 teaspoon salt
2/3 cup vegetable oil
1 (6-ounce) can frozen tangerine juice
    concentrate, thawed
1/2 cup orange juice
2 eggs
1 tablespoon grated orange rind
2 teaspoons vanilla extract
2 cups semisweet chocolate chips

Blend oil, tangerine juice concentrate, orange juice, eggs, orange rind and vanilla in bowl. Mix flour, sugar, brown sugar, baking powder, baking soda and salt together in large bowl. Make well in center of flour mixture. Add orange juice mixture. Stir just until moistened. Stir in chocolate chips. Spoon batter into greased 2½-inch muffin cups. Bake at 400 degrees for 15 to 20 minutes or until wooden pick inserted in center of muffin comes out clean. Cool for 5 minutes. Remove to wire rack to cool completely. Store at room temperature in airtight container.

Yield: 2 dozen

OUTDOOR LORE

Carry picnic foods in several small baskets rather than in one large basket for easier packing and transporting.

Keep a bag of picnic essentials handy to go at a moment's notice. Fill with salt and pepper packets, bottle opener, premoistened towelettes, earplugs and trash bags; replenish after each outing.

VICTORY DESSERT PIZZA

1½ cups flour
1/2 cup confectioners' sugar
3/4 cup butter, melted
8 ounces cream cheese, softened
1/2 cup sugar
1/4 teaspoon vanilla extract
Segments of 2 oranges and 2 tangerines
1 banana, sliced
1/2 cup sliced strawberries
1/2 cup blueberries
1/4 cup sugar
2 tablespoons cornstarch
1 cup orange juice

Combine flour and confectioners' sugar in bowl. Add butter; mix well. Pat into 11-inch tart pan with removable bottom. Prick surface with fork. Bake at 350 degrees for 10 to 15 minutes. Let stand until cool. Combine cream cheese, ½ cup sugar and vanilla in bowl; mix well. Spread over cooled crust. Arrange fruit over cream cheese. Combine ¼ cup sugar, cornstarch and orange juice in small saucepan. Cook over medium heat until thickened, stirring constantly. Spoon over fruit. Chill in refrigerator.

Yield: 12 servings

FOUR-FRUIT PUNCH

1 (46-ounce) can pineapple juice
1 (6-ounce) can frozen orange juice
    concentrate
1 (6-ounce) can frozen lemonade concentrate
1 (6-ounce) can frozen white grape juice
    concentrate

Combine pineapple juice, orange juice concentrate, lemonade concentrate and grape juice concentrate in 1-gallon jug; mix well. Add enough water to fill jug; mix well. Chill until serving time.

Yield: 10 servings

OKTOBERFEST TAILGATE PARTY

Pumpernickel Bites

Potted Franks   German Coleslaw

Sauerkraut Salad

German Potato Salad

Swiss Cheese Bread

Meat Loaf Swirl

Fresh Apple Cake

Peanut Clusters   Apple Cider

Fall is the perfect time for tailgating, and German foods are perfect for fall. Hearty and spicy, this tailgate menu is a great prelude to whatever activities follow.

PUMPERNICKEL BITES

8 ounces cream cheese, softened
1 envelope Italian salad dressing mix
1 loaf cocktail pumpernickel bread
2 cucumbers, thinly sliced

Combine cream cheese and salad dressing mix in bowl. Spread on bread slices. Top each with cucumber slice.

Yield: 20 appetizers

POTTED FRANKS

1 (10-ounce) jar currant jelly
½ cup prepared mustard
1 tablespoon prepared horseradish
1 pound frankfurters

Melt jelly in slow cooker. Stir in mustard and horseradish. Cut frankfurters into 1-inch pieces. Add to slow cooker. Cook on High until heated through, stirring occasionally.

Yield: 60 servings

GERMAN COLESLAW

8 cups shredded cabbage
2 green bell peppers, finely chopped
1 red bell pepper, finely chopped
4 medium onions, finely chopped
1⅓ cups cider vinegar
2½ cups sugar
1 teaspoon celery seed
1½ teaspoons each mustard seed and salt
½ teaspoon turmeric

Combine cabbage, bell peppers and onions in bowl; mix well. Combine vinegar and remaining ingredients in saucepan. Bring to a boil. Pour over cabbage mixture. Chill, covered, for 24 hours or longer.

Yield: 12 cups

SAUERKRAUT SALAD

2 (16-ounce) cans sauerkraut
1 green bell pepper, chopped
1 cup chopped onion
1 cup chopped celery
1 (8-ounce) can sliced water chestnuts, drained
1 (4-ounce) jar chopped pimentos, drained
⅓ cup each water and vegetable oil
⅔ cup vinegar
1½ cups sugar

Rinse and drain sauerkraut. Combine with green pepper, onion, celery, water chestnuts and pimentos in salad bowl. Combine water, oil, vinegar and sugar in saucepan. Heat to the simmering point, stirring to dissolve sugar. Add to vegetables; mix well. Chill for several hours to overnight.

Yield: 10 servings

German Potato Salad

9 medium potatoes
Salt to taste
6 slices bacon
¾ cup chopped onion
2 tablespoons flour
2 tablespoons sugar
2 teaspoons salt
½ teaspoon celery seed
Dash of pepper
¾ cup water
⅓ cup vinegar

Scrub and pare potatoes. Place in 1 inch salted water in saucepan. Cook for 30 to 35 minutes or until tender. Drain; set aside. Brown bacon in skillet; remove bacon to paper towels to drain. Add onion to bacon drippings. Cook until golden brown. Stir in flour, sugar, 2 teaspoons salt, celery seed and pepper. Remove from heat. Stir in water and vinegar. Bring to a boil. Cook for 1 minute, stirring constantly. Slice potatoes. Stir into hot mixture. Stir in crumbled bacon.

Yield: 8 servings

Swiss Cheese Bread

1 cup butter or margarine
½ teaspoon prepared mustard
1 tablespoon lemon juice
1 tablespoon poppy seed
½ teaspoon Beau Monde seasoning
2 tablespoons grated onion
1 (1-pound) loaf French bread
8 ounces sliced Swiss cheese

Combine butter, mustard, lemon juice, poppy seed, Beau Monde seasoning and onion in saucepan. Heat until butter melts, stirring frequently. Cut crisscross pattern on top of bread. Drizzle butter mixture between cuts. Place cheese between cuts. Wrap in foil. Bake at 350 degrees for 30 minutes.

Yield: 12 servings

Meat Loaf Swirl

1 (10-ounce) package frozen
   chopped broccoli
2 pounds ground beef
2 eggs
¾ cup soft bread crumbs
¼ cup catsup
¼ cup milk
2 packages dry onion soup mix
½ teaspoon salt
¼ teaspoon pepper
¼ teaspoon dried oregano
½ cup chopped tomatoes
1 (3-ounce) package smoked ham
3 slices mozzarella cheese
3 slices American cheese

Rinse frozen broccoli under cold running water to separate; drain. Combine ground beef, eggs, bread crumbs, catsup, milk, onion soup mix, salt, pepper and oregano in bowl; mix well. Pat into 10×12-inch rectangle on 15×18-inch piece of foil. Layer broccoli, tomatoes and ham to within ½ inch of edges. Roll up ground beef rectangle carefully, beginning at short end and using foil to lift. Press edge and ends to seal. Place on rack in shallow baking pan. Bake at 350 degrees for 1 hour. Cut cheese slices diagonally into halves. Overlap cheeses on top of loaf. Bake for 1 minute or until cheeses begin to melt. Garnish with parsley and pimento if desired. Center of meat loaf may be slightly pink due to ham.

Yield: 8 to 12 servings

FRESH APPLE CAKE

3 cups flour
1 teaspoon salt
1 teaspoon baking soda
1 teaspoon cinnamon
1/4 teaspoon ginger
1/4 teaspoon nutmeg
1/4 teaspoon cloves
1/4 teaspoon allspice
2 cups sugar
1 1/4 cups corn oil
2 eggs
1 teaspoon vanilla extract
3 large apples, peeled, finely chopped

Mix flour, salt, baking soda and spices together in bowl. Beat sugar, oil, eggs and vanilla in bowl. Add flour mixture; mix well. Batter will be stiff. Stir in apples. Pour into greased 9×13-inch cake pan. Bake at 350 degrees for 45 minutes.

Yield: 12 servings

PEANUT CLUSTERS

8 ounces almond bark
1 cup dry-roasted peanuts
1 cup Cheerios
1 cup broken pretzels

Place almond bark in glass bowl. Microwave on High for 60 seconds or until melted. Stir in peanuts, Cheerios and pretzels. Drop by teaspoonfuls onto waxed paper. Let stand until cool.

Yield: 3 to 4 servings

OUTDOOR LORE

Pick up store-bought foods for no-fuss picnics. Pack fruit, cheese and French baguettes; gingersnaps, tart apples, paté and cream cheese; hard rolls, deli roast beef and pasta salad.

TAILGATE BARBECUE

Chili Cheese Ball

Sesame-Cheese Bites

Cornfetti   Celery Seed Slaw

Tailgate Barbecue

Calico Beans   Baked Poato Salad

Corn Light Bread

Chocolate Chess Pies

Lemonade Tea Punch

Take these make-ahead treats to your next tailgate picnic right in their baking dishes. Wrap slow cookers and casseroles in layers of newspaper to keep warm. Use the newspaper as tablecloths when you arrive and for cleanup later. Serve punch in mason jars, and use pie tin plates and paper towel napkins.

CHILI CHEESE BALL

16 ounces Velveeta cheese, at room
   temperature
8 ounces cream cheese, at room temperature
1/2 cup chopped nuts
1/4 teaspoon garlic powder
Dash of salt
Chili powder to taste

Combine Velveeta cheese and cream cheese in mixer bowl. Beat until smooth and blended. Add nuts, garlic powder and salt; mix well. Shape into ball. Coat with chili powder. Serve with crackers.

Yield: 1 cheese ball

SESAME-CHEESE BITES

2 cups baking mix
½ cup club soda
½ cup shredded Cheddar cheese
3 tablespoons melted butter or margarine
Sesame seed to taste

Combine baking mix, club soda and cheese in bowl; mix well. Beat vigorously for 20 strokes. Shape into ball on floured surface. Knead 5 times. Roll into 10×16-inch rectangle. Cut into 2-inch squares; cut diagonally into halves. Brush with butter. Sprinkle with sesame seed. Place on ungreased baking sheet. Bake in preheated 450-degree oven for 8 minutes or until brown.

Yield: 80 servings

CORNFETTI

2 (12-ounce) cans whole kernel corn, drained
½ cup sweet pickle relish
¼ cup chopped green bell pepper
2 tablespoons minced onion
2 tablespoons chopped pimento
1 teaspoon salt
¼ cup Italian salad dressing

Combine corn, pickle relish, green pepper, onion, pimento and salt in bowl; mix well. Add salad dressing; toss to mix. Chill, covered, for 4 hours.

Yield: 12 servings

OUTDOOR LORE

Carry a slow-cooker-full-of-ribs to the tailgate. The night before, cook 3 pounds country-style pork ribs with 1 bottle of barbecue sauce and enough water to cover in slow cooker on Low for 9 to 10 hours.

CELERY SEED SLAW

1 large head cabbage, shredded
1 onion, chopped
¾ cup sugar
1 cup vinegar
1 cup mayonnaise
¼ cup vegetable oil
1 tablespoon sugar
1 tablespoon dry mustard
1 teaspoon celery seed
1 tablespoon salt

Combine cabbage and onion in large bowl. Sprinkle with ¾ cup sugar. Combine vinegar, mayonnaise, oil, 1 tablespoon sugar, dry mustard, celery seed and salt in saucepan. Bring to a boil. Pour over cabbage mixture; mix well. Chill, covered, in refrigerator for 3 hours or longer. May store in covered container in refrigerator.

Yield: 12 servings

TAILGATE BARBECUE

1 (5-pound) boneless beef or pork roast
⅓ cup packed brown sugar
1 cup water
2 cups catsup
2 tablespoons prepared mustard
¼ cup Worcestershire sauce
3 tablespoons brown sugar
2 tablespoons liquid smoke
1 (10-ounce) can cola
⅛ teaspoon Tabasco sauce

Rub roast with ⅓ cup brown sugar. Place in roasting pan. Add water. Bake, covered, at 225 degrees for 6 to 8 hours or until tender. Let stand until cool. Trim fat; shred roast. Combine catsup, mustard, Worcestershire sauce, 3 tablespoons brown sugar, liquid smoke, cola and Tabasco sauce in large saucepan. Add roast. Simmer for 1 hour, stirring occasionally.

Yield: 12 servings

CALICO BEANS

12 ounces ground beef
1 large onion, chopped
12 ounces sliced bacon, crisp-fried, crumbled
1 (16-ounce) can brick-oven baked beans
1 (16-ounce) can lima beans, drained
1 (16-ounce) can butter beans, drained
1 (16-ounce) can kidney beans, drained
½ cup packed brown sugar
½ cup catsup
2 tablespoons vinegar
1 tablespoon prepared mustard
1 tablespoon bacon drippings

Brown ground beef with onion in skillet, stirring mixture frequently; drain. Combine with bacon in large baking pan. Add beans; mix gently. Combine brown sugar, catsup, vinegar and mustard in saucepan. Simmer for 15 minutes. Add to bean mixture; mix well. Drizzle with bacon drippings. Bake at 350 degrees for 35 to 40 minutes or until bubbly.

Yield: 12 servings

BAKED POTATO SALAD

8 medium potatoes, cooked, chopped
8 ounces American cheese, chopped
¼ cup chopped onion
¼ cup chopped celery
8 ounces bacon, crisp-fried, crumbled
1 cup mayonnaise
Salt and pepper to taste
1 cup butter cracker crumbs

Combine potatoes, cheese, onion, celery, bacon, mayonnaise, salt and pepper in bowl; mix well. Spoon into buttered 9×13-inch baking pan. Sprinkle buttered crumbs on top. Bake at 350 degrees for 55 minutes.

Yield: 8 to 12 servings

CORN LIGHT BREAD

3 cups self-rising cornmeal
1 cup sugar
¾ cup flour
3 cups buttermilk
½ cup vegetable oil

Combine cornmeal, sugar and flour in bowl. Stir in mixture of buttermilk and oil. Pour into 2 greased 5×9-inch loaf pans. Bake at 350 degrees for 45 minutes or until loaves test done. Remove to wire rack to cool. Serve warm or cold.

Yield: 2 loaves

CHOCOLATE CHESS PIES

½ cup melted margarine
3 cups sugar
½ cup baking cocoa
4 eggs, beaten
2 teaspoons vanilla extract
1 (12-ounce) can evaporated milk
2 unbaked (9-inch) pie shells

Combine first 6 ingredients in bowl in order listed, mixing well after each addition. Pour into pie shells. Bake at 300 degrees for 1 hour.

Yield: 12 servings

LEMONADE TEA PUNCH

2 (10-ounce) packages frozen strawberries, thawed
2 (6-ounce) cans frozen lemonade concentrate, thawed
1 cup sugar
1 cup instant tea
12 cups water

Combine first 4 ingredients in blender container. Process on High until blended. Pour into pitcher. Add water. Serve over ice.

Yield: 12 servings

Campfire Cooking

Surprisingly enough, grown-ups, who think nothing of preparing a gourmet extravaganza complete with a flaming dessert, pale at the thought of whipping up dinner over a campfire.

Admittedly, preparing a meal over an outdoor fire is a different matter than flambéing Cherries Jubilee. But with a little confidence, and this chapter, you can become an accomplished campfire chef with surprising ease.

Several menus give you an idea of the possibilities, including a *Campfire Breakfast* that will get your day off to a great start. *The Backpacker's Lunch*—no freeze-dried soup and trail mix here—includes a salad that can be assembled on the trail. And if you thought baked goodies were impossible in the great outdoors, take a look at the bread and cobbler in our *Dutch Oven Dinner*. (You'll find Dutch Oven instructions in the *Outdoor Essentials* at the back of the book.)

Our *Potless-Luck Supper* is cooked, completely in mess-free foil containers. And for a fun, economical treat, try our *Hobo Feast*.

Remember, most campfire recipes came about through someone's on-the-spot improvisation. The key to success when cooking in the wild is to relax and have fun—and to try anything once.

CAMPFIRE BREAKFAST

Creole Scramble, Rice Scramble or
Bacon and Egg Burritos

Camper's Apples

Muffins in Orange Cups,
French Toast Crunch or
Hawaiian Delights

Banana Shake or Orange Juice

*At no place or time does food taste
better than outdoors early in the morning.
These suggestions will get the whole
camp up and going.*

CREOLE SCRAMBLE

1 pound bacon, chopped
3 cups canned whole kernel corn, drained
1 cup chopped green bell pepper
18 eggs, beaten
Salt and pepper to taste

Fry bacon in skillet until crisp; drain. Combine bacon, corn and green pepper in skillet. Sauté until green pepper is tender. Beat eggs with salt and pepper in bowl. Pour into skillet. Cook until eggs are set, stirring gently frequently.

Yield: 12 servings

RICE SCRAMBLE

3 cups water
Salt to taste
3 cups minute rice
12 eggs
¼ cup water
1 tablespoon instant minced onion
2 cups shredded Monterey Jack cheese

Bring 3 cups water with salt to a boil in skillet. Stir in rice; cover and remove from heat. Let stand for 5 minutes. Beat eggs with ¼ cup water in bowl. Stir in onion and cheese. Pour into hot skillet. Cook until eggs are set, turning frequently. Add the rice; mix well.

Yield: 12 servings

BACON AND EGG BURRITOS

3 pounds bacon, chopped
3 (16-ounce) cans potatoes, drained, sliced
24 eggs, beaten
2 cups milk
2 pounds Monterey Jack cheese, shredded
24 flour tortillas

Cook bacon in large heavy skillet over hot coals until crisp; drain, reserving drippings. Set bacon aside. Brown potatoes in a small amount of reserved drippings in skillet; remove potatoes and set aside. Heat desired amount of reserved drippings in skillet. Beat eggs with milk in bowl. Add to skillet. Cook until eggs are set, stirring frequently. Add bacon, potatoes and cheese. Cook until cheese melts, stirring constantly. Spoon onto tortillas; roll to enclose filling. Place on plates. Serve with salsa.

Yield: 24 servings

CAMPER'S APPLES

12 (or more) apples, sliced
¼ cup butter
1 cup raisins
¼ cup packed brown sugar
1 tablespoon cinnamon

Combine apples, butter, raisins, brown sugar and cinnamon in large heavy skillet; mix well. Cook over hot coals for 15 minutes or until apples are tender, stirring occasionally. May divide ingredients into portions, seal in individual foil packets and bake in hot coals.

Yield: 12 servings

MUFFINS IN ORANGE CUPS

6 oranges
2 (7-ounce) packages muffin mix

Cut oranges into halves. Scoop out orange pulp and reserve for another purpose; reserve shells. Prepare muffin mix using package directions. Fill orange shells ½ full. Wrap individually in foil. Place in hot coals. Bake for 5 to 10 minutes or until muffins test done.

Yield: 12 servings

FRENCH TOAST CRUNCH

12 slices bread
4 eggs, beaten
2 cups crushed wheat flakes cereal
½ cup butter

Trim crusts from bread if desired; cut slices into halves. Dip into beaten eggs in bowl; coat with cereal. Brown in butter in heavy skillet over hot coals. Serve with maple syrup or jam.

Yield: 12 servings

HAWAIIAN DELIGHTS

6 glazed doughnuts
6 pineapple slices
6 tablespoons brown sugar

Split each doughnut into 2 layers. Place pineapple slices between layers. Place each doughnut sandwich on 12×12-inch piece of foil. Fill doughnut holes with brown sugar. Double-fold sides and ends of foil, sealing tightly. Place on grill over hot coals. Cook for 10 minutes on each side. Open foil carefully.

Yield: 6 servings

BANANA SHAKE

6 bananas, mashed
2 tablespoons lemon juice
1 tablespoon vanilla extract
6 cups milk

Combine all ingredients in large jar. Cover jar tightly. Shake until smooth. Pour into cups.

Yield: 12 servings

WHITEWATER CANOEING FEAST

Who says camping fare can't be elegant. Bake potatoes and cored apples filled with butter, sugar, cinnamon and red hot cinnamon candies in foil in coals while grilling steaks on grill. Mix up salad ingredients in large plastic bag and enjoy.

DUTCH OVEN DINNER

Campers' Salad

**Pork Chops Plus or
Glazed Cornish Hens**

Vegetable Medley

Dutch Oven-Baked Bread

**Upside-Down Cake or
Dutch Oven Cobbler**

*Dutch oven cooking is easy and requires
less watching than most outdoor cookery.
Just stack your ovens (see page 116) to cook
a whole meal—even a fancy dinner.*

CAMPERS' SALAD

1 cup sugar
1 cup cider vinegar
¼ cup chili sauce
¼ cup vegetable oil
1 green bell pepper, finely chopped
1 onion, finely chopped
1 (2-ounce) can chopped pimento
6 stalks celery, finely chopped
4 carrots, finely chopped
2 heads lettuce, shredded

Combine sugar, vinegar, chili sauce and oil in
bowl; mix until sugar dissolves. Add chopped vegetables; mix well. Pour desired amount of dressing
over lettuce in salad bowl; toss lightly to coat.

Yield: 8 servings

PORK CHOPS PLUS

8 pork chops
1 cup uncooked rice
8 thick onion slices
8 thick tomato slices
4 thick green bell pepper slices
¼ teaspoon marjoram
¼ teaspoon thyme
Salt and pepper to taste
2 (10-ounce) cans bouillon

Preheat enough charcoal briquettes to cover top
and bottom of Dutch oven, leaving 2 inches
between coals. One briquette generates 40
degrees of heat. Preheat Dutch oven over hot
coals. Brown pork chops on both sides; arrange in
oven. Sprinkle rice into spaces between pork
chops. Top each pork chop with slice of onion,
tomato and green pepper. Sprinkle with seasonings. Pour bouillon over top. Place covered Dutch
oven in coals; top with coals. Bake for 1 hour or
until chops and rice are tender.

Yield: 8 servings

GLAZED CORNISH HENS

3 cups apricot-pineapple jam
3 cups apple juice
8 Cornish hens, split, flattened
Salt to taste

Preheat 20 to 22 charcoal briquettes. Preheat
large Dutch oven over coals. Blend jam and apple
juice in bowl. Layer 4 hens, half the jam mixture,
remaining hens and remaining jam mixture in
Dutch oven. Sprinkle with salt. Place covered
oven over 8 coals; top with remaining coals. Bake
for 45 minutes or until hens are tender, turning
hens occasionally.

Yield: 8 servings

VEGETABLE MEDLEY

6 small zucchini, sliced
6 carrots, sliced
2 cups broccoli flowerets
24 mushrooms, sliced
½ teaspoon rosemary
⅛ teaspoon thyme
1 cup water
¼ cup butter
½ cup beef broth
½ cup sunflower seed
Salt and pepper to taste

Preheat 25 charcoal briquettes. Preheat large Dutch oven over coals. Combine zucchini, carrots, broccoli and mushrooms in large bowl. Add rosemary and thyme; toss to coat. Combine water, butter and broth in Dutch oven. Add vegetables. Place covered oven over 10 coals; top with remaining coals. Bake for 20 minutes or until vegetables are tender-crisp. Sprinkle with sunflower seed, salt and pepper.

Yield: 8 servings

DUTCH OVEN-BAKED BREAD

1 package hot roll mix
1 (12-ounce) can warm club soda
2 tablespoons cornmeal

Prepare hot roll mix using package directions and substituting equivalent amount of warm club soda for water. Knead on floured surface until smooth and elastic. Place in greased bowl, turning to grease surface. Let rise, covered, for 1 hour or until doubled in bulk. Shape into 2 loaves. Place in greased Dutch oven sprinkled with cornmeal. Let rise, covered, for 1 hour. Preheat 20 charcoal briquettes. Cut diagonal slashes in loaves; sprinkle with water. Place covered Dutch oven over half the coals; top with remaining coals. Bake for 40 minutes or until loaves test done, checking every 20 minutes. Remove several coals if bread is baking too fast.

Yield: 2 loaves

UPSIDE-DOWN CAKE

1 (16-ounce) can sliced pineapple
2 tablespoons margarine
1 small jar maraschino cherries
½ cup packed brown sugar
1 (2-layer) package yellow cake mix

Drain pineapple, reserving juice. Line Dutch oven with foil. Grease foil with margarine. Arrange pineapple and cherries on foil. Sprinkle brown sugar and 3 tablespoons reserved juice over fruit. Prepare cake mix using package directions. Pour over fruit. Place cover on Dutch oven. Place 1 inch above hot coals. Top with hot coals. Bake for 25 to 30 minutes or until cake tests done. Cool for 10 minutes. Invert onto platter. Peel off foil.

Yield: 6 to 8 servings

DUTCH OVEN COBBLER

1 (21-ounce) can cherry pie filling
¼ cup sugar
1 (12-ounce) package baking mix
¼ cup butter, melted
2 tablespoons cinnamon-sugar

Preheat 20 charcoal briquettes. Line Dutch oven with foil. Preheat Dutch oven near coals. Combine pie filling and sugar in oven. Heat over 8 coals until mixture comes to a boil. Combine baking mix and enough water to make soft dough in bowl. Drop by spoonfuls over cherry mixture. Cover and top with remaining coals. Bake for 15 to 20 minutes or until golden brown. Brush with butter; sprinkle with cinnamon-sugar.

Yield: 8 servings

OUTDOOR LORE

If several families are camping together, have each be responsible for planning and preparing a meal. This adds variety and spreads the work around.

BACKPACKER'S LUNCH

Apple Slices

Trail Salad

Hiker's Treats

**S'Mores and More or
Picnic Chocolate Fondue**

Easy to carry and delicious to eat, these trail-lover's treats include portables that are ready to heat when you get to the top. Mix salad in disposable cups.

APPLE SLICES

8 ounces cream cheese, softened
1/3 cup confectioners' sugar
1/4 cup chopped pecans
4 large Delicious apples

Combine cream cheese, confectioners' sugar and pecans in bowl; mix well. Cut each unpeeled apple into 8 wedges. Spread cream cheese mixture on apples. Serve immediately. May place apple wedges in mixture of lemon juice and water to prevent browning if apples are prepared in advance.

Yield: 8 to 10 servings

TRAIL SALAD

3 (20-ounce) cans fruit cocktail
3 bananas, sliced
1 (8-ounce) package miniature marshmallows

Drain fruit cocktail; spoon into disposable cups. Add bananas and marshmallows; mix gently.

Yield: 8 servings

HIKER'S TREATS

1 pound bologna, chopped
1 pound Cheddar cheese, chopped
1 cup pickle relish
1 cup chopped onion
10 tablespoons catsup
10 teaspoons prepared mustard
10 hot dog buns

Mix bologna, cheese, relish, onion, catsup and mustard in bowl. Spoon into hot dog buns. Wrap each bun in foil, sealing tightly. Place on grill over hot coals. Cook for 10 minutes or until cheese melts, turning occasionally.

Yield: 10 servings

S'MORES AND MORE

3 (1½-ounce) milk chocolate bars
18 graham crackers
9 large marshmallows

Break each chocolate bar into thirds. Place on 9 graham crackers. Toast marshmallows on sticks over hot coals until golden; place marshmallows on chocolate. Top with remaining graham crackers; press together gently. May substitute peanut butter for chocolate.

Yield: 9 servings

PICNIC CHOCOLATE FONDUE

16 ounces semisweet chocolate chips
1½ cups whipping cream

Melt chocolate chips in skillet over very low coals. Stir in whipping cream. Dip banana chunks, orange segments or other fruit into fondue with skewers or sticks.

Yield: 2 cups

HOBO FEAST

**Potatoes and Franks or
Hobo Hamburger**

**Brown Bear in an Orchard or
Mock Angel Food Cake**

Watermelon or other fresh fruit

*With stars as the candles and pine needles
for the tablecloth, any food will be a
banquet. Our menu is economical and
easy as well as delicious.*

POTATOES AND FRANKS

*1 cup chopped onion
1½ cups chopped green bell pepper
2 tablespoons butter
2 (5½-ounce) packages au gratin potatoes with
   sauce mix
4½ cups water
1⅓ cups milk
¼ cup chopped parsley
¼ cup butter
2 tablespoons chili sauce
1 tablespoon prepared mustard
1 cup shredded Cheddar cheese
6 frankfurters, sliced*

Sauté onion and green pepper in 2 tablespoons butter in heavy skillet over medium coals. Add potatoes, sauce mix, water, milk, parsley and ¼ cup butter; mix well. Bring to a boil, stirring frequently. Cook, covered, for 20 minutes. Stir in chili sauce and mustard. Sprinkle cheese over top. Arrange frankfurters spoke-fashion on top. Cook, covered, for 10 minutes longer or until heated through.

Yield: 8 servings

HOBO HAMBURGER

*1 large carrot
1 large baking potato
4 ounces ground beef
1 teaspoon salt
1 teaspoon pepper
1 teaspoon Worcestershire sauce*

Peel carrot and potato; slice into thin rounds. Shape ground beef into patty. Layer ground beef patty, carrot and potato in center of 20-inch square heavy-duty foil. Sprinkle with salt, pepper and Worcestershire sauce. Bring 2 sides of foil together; roll or fold until foil touches food. Fold ends toward center and flatten to seal. Place packet on hot coals. Cook for 7 to 10 minutes on each side. Make as many pouches as needed.

Yield: 1 serving

BROWN BEAR IN AN ORCHARD

*1 (20-ounce) can applesauce
1 (14-ounce) package gingerbread mix*

Heat applesauce in Dutch oven over hot coals. Prepare gingerbread mix using package directions. Pour over hot applesauce. Cover Dutch oven. Place in hot coals. Bake for 20 to 30 minutes or until gingerbread tests done. Serve with whipped cream.

Yield: 8 to 10 servings

MOCK ANGEL FOOD CAKE

*1 loaf unsliced white bread
1 (15-ounce) can sweetened condensed milk
1 package shredded coconut*

Trim crust from loaf; cut bread into pieces. Dip pieces into condensed milk; roll in coconut. Insert stick into bread. Toast over hot coals until golden brown, turning frequently to brown evenly.

Yield: 10 to 15 servings

A POTLESS-LUCK SUPPER

Hot Knapsack Salad

Chicken-in-the-Garden or
Salmon-Zucchini Bundles

Cheesy French Bread

Corn-on-the-Cob

Grilled Potatoes

Campfire Cupcakes or Banana Boats

Campfire cooking is a snap with foil cooking, and there is no cleanup. Cook in foil packets, and serve in the cooking pouch. You can even make the packets up at home for extra-easy transporting.

HOT KNAPSACK SALAD

2 bananas
2 plums
2 peaches
1 (8-ounce) can pineapple, drained
¼ cup packed brown sugar
¼ cup butter
4 teaspoons lemon juice

Cut fresh fruit into chunks; divide among 4 pieces of heavy-duty foil. Add ¼ of pineapple, brown sugar, butter and lemon juice to each fruit portion. Fold foil, sealing tightly. Attach packets to sticks, insert sticks through packets or place packets on grill. Cook over medium coals for 10 minutes or until heated through.

Yield: 4 servings

CHICKEN-IN-THE-GARDEN

1 medium tomato, peeled
1 onion, peeled
3 fresh mushrooms
3 green bell pepper rings
1 small potato
1 large chicken breast
1 teaspoon Worcestershire sauce
Garlic salt, pepper and paprika to taste
1 teaspoon margarine
1 tablespoon honey

Place vegetables in center of 20-inch piece of heavy-duty foil. Place chicken in vegetables. Sprinkle with Worcestershire sauce, garlic salt, pepper and paprika. Dot with margarine; drizzle honey over all. Fold and seal foil tightly. Cook over hot coals for 1½ hours, turning every 20 minutes. May bake at 450 degrees for 1 hour. Make as many packets as needed.

Yield: 1 serving

SALMON-ZUCCHINI BUNDLES

4 (6-ounce) salmon steaks
1 can tomato soup
¼ teaspoon garlic powder
1 medium zucchini, thinly sliced
¼ cup grated Parmesan cheese

Cut four 14-inch squares heavy-duty foil. Place 1 salmon steak in center of each. Combine soup, garlic powder, zucchini and cheese in bowl; mix well. Spoon over salmon. Fold and seal foil tightly. Place on grill 4 inches above hot coals. Cook for 25 minutes.

Yield: 4 servings

CHEESY FRENCH BREAD

1 large loaf French bread
2 cups shredded mozzarella cheese
2 (4-ounce) cans sliced mushrooms, drained
2 tablespoons minced onion
2 tablespoons poppy seed
1 cup melted margarine
1 teaspoon lemon juice
1 teaspoon garlic salt

Slice French bread into 1-inch slices to but not through bottom of loaf. Place on large sheet heavy-duty foil. Spoon mixture of cheese and mushrooms between slices. Combine onion, poppy seed, margarine, lemon juice and garlic salt in bowl; mix well. Drizzle over loaf. Fold and seal foil tightly. Place on grill over medium coals. Cook for 15 minutes or until cheese melts, turning frequently.

Yield: 8 to 10 servings

CORN-ON-THE-COB

½ cup butter, softened
¼ cup grated Parmesan cheese
¼ cup mayonnaise
1 tablespoon instant minced onion
¼ teaspoon garlic powder
¼ teaspoon white pepper
1 or 2 ears of corn per person

Combine butter, cheese, mayonnaise, onion, garlic powder and white pepper in mixer bowl. Beat for 2 to 3 minutes or until light and creamy. Chill, covered, for 1 hour or longer. Spread corn generously with butter mixture; wrap ears individually in foil. Place on grill over low coals. Grill for 20 minutes, turning frequently.

Yield: variable

GRILLED POTATOES

3 or 4 medium potatoes
3 slices crisp-fried bacon, crumbled
8 ounces American cheese, cubed
1 medium onion, chopped
1 cup margarine

Peel and thinly slice potatoes. Place on large sheet heavy-duty foil. Layer bacon, cheese and onion over potatoes. Dot with margarine. Fold and seal foil tightly. Place on grill over medium coals. Cook for 1 hour or until potatoes are tender, turning occasionally.

Yield: 5 to 6 servings

CAMPFIRE CUPCAKES

12 to 15 oranges
1 (2-layer) package favorite flavor cake mix

Cut oranges into halves. Scoop out pulp to form shells; reserve pulp for another purpose. Prepare cake mix using package directions. Fill each orange shell ⅔ full. Wrap each orange shell loosely in foil. Place over medium coals. Bake for 20 minutes or until cake tests done. Remove from foil.

Yield: 24 to 30 cupcakes

BANANA BOATS

4 bananas
40 miniature marshmallows
4 milk chocolate bars, broken

Peel back 1 section banana peel from each banana; do not remove. Cut wedge-shaped section lengthwise from each banana. Place marshmallows and chocolate in bananas. Replace peels; wrap each banana tightly in heavy-duty foil. Place in coals or on grill over coals. Bake for 3 minutes or until chocolate and marshmallows are melted.

Yield: 4 servings

BEEF STROGANOFF

2 large round steaks, cubed
3 tablespoons vegetable oil
2 large onions, chopped
2 large packages fresh mushrooms, sliced
2 cans cream of mushroom soup
½ cup sour cream

Brown steaks in hot oil in large cast-iron skillet over red-hot coals. Add onions and mushrooms. Cook until tender. Add soup. Cook, covered, for 30 to 45 minutes or until steak is tender. Add sour cream. Cook for 20 minutes longer. Serve over hot cooked rice.

Yield: 8 to 10 servings

LEMONY CHUCK ROAST

1 (4-pound) beef chuck roast, 1½ inches thick
1 teaspoon grated lemon rind
½ cup lemon juice
⅓ cup vegetable oil
2 tablespoons sliced green onions and tops
4 teaspoons sugar
1½ teaspoons salt
1 teaspoon Worcestershire sauce
1 teaspoon prepared mustard
⅛ teaspoon pepper

Score fat edges of roast; place in shallow 9x13-inch baking dish. Combine remaining ingredients in bowl; mix well. Pour over roast. Marinate, covered, at room temperature for 3 hours or in refrigerator overnight, turning roast occasionally. Drain, reserving marinade. Pat roast dry with paper towel; place on grill over medium-hot coals. Grill for 17 to 20 minutes on each side for rare to medium-rare. Heat reserved marinade on grill. Slice roast thin. Serve with hot marinade.

Yield: 12 servings

DUTCH OVEN BEEF STEW

2 to 3 pounds stew beef
3 tablespoons shortening
Salt and pepper to taste
1 (29-ounce) can stewed tomatoes
6 to 8 carrots, peeled, sliced
1 large onion, sliced
4 to 6 large potatoes, cut into chunks
2 or 3 stalks celery, sliced
1 (20-ounce) can green beans
1 (20-ounce) can corn
2 beef bouillon cubes
½ cup catsup

Brown beef in shortening in Dutch oven. Add remaining ingredients; mix well. Place covered Dutch oven on coals or charcoal briquettes. Use 12 to 14 coals on bottom and 6 to 8 coals on lid. Cook for 3 to 4 hours or until beef is tender.

Yield: 10 to 12 servings

CAMPFIRE STEW

1 (3-pound) chuck roast
1 cup flour
2 teaspoons salt
1 teaspoon pepper
½ cup vegetable oil
6 potatoes, cubed
6 carrots, sliced
2 onions, sliced
2 stalks celery, sliced
1 bay leaf
3 cups water

Trim roast; cut into bite-sized pieces. Dredge in mixture of flour, salt and pepper to coat. Brown in hot oil in Dutch oven over hot coals, stirring frequently. Add remaining ingredients; mix well. Cook over hot coals for 4 hours or until roast and vegetables are tender, stirring occasionally and adding additional water if necessary.

Yield: 15 servings

DEVIL'S DELIGHT CHILI

5 slices bacon
8 ounces Italian sausage links, sliced
2 medium onions, chopped
1 small green bell pepper, chopped
1½ pounds beef chuck steak, chopped
1 clove of garlic, minced
2 jalapeño peppers, chopped
2 dried red chili peppers, crumbled
1 to 1½ tablespoons chili powder
½ teaspoon crushed oregano
½ teaspoon salt
1 (12-ounce) can tomato paste
2½ cups water
1 (16-ounce) can pinto beans, drained
1 (16-ounce) can garbanzo beans, drained

Brown bacon in Dutch oven over hot coals until crisp; drain, reserving drippings. Crumble bacon. Brown sausage in bacon drippings. Drain, reserving 2 tablespoons drippings; set sausage aside. Cook onions, green pepper, steak and garlic in pan drippings until steak is brown. Add bacon, sausage, jalapeño peppers, chili peppers, chili powder, oregano and salt; mix well. Stir in tomato paste and water. Bring to a boil; reduce heat. Simmer, covered, for 1½ hours, stirring occasionally. Stir in pinto beans and garbanzo beans. Simmer, covered, for 30 minutes longer.

Yield: 8 servings

BEACH STEAK SANDWICH

2 tablespoons butter, softened
Several slices eye-of-round steak
1 French roll, split

Build campfire on the beach. Melt butter in cast-iron skillet over hot coals. Add steak. Cook until done to taste. Brush roll with additional butter. Pile steak between roll.

Yield: 1 serving

BEEFY NOODLES

3 pounds ground beef
1¼ cups margarine
1 onion, chopped
1 green bell pepper, chopped
2 cups chopped celery
2 (20-ounce) cans tomatoes
Salt and pepper to taste
1 (16-ounce) package noodles

Brown ground beef in margarine in Dutch oven over medium coals, stirring until crumbly. Add onion, green pepper and celery. Sauté until tender. Stir in tomatoes, salt and pepper. Bring to a boil. Add noodles. Cook for 15 minutes, adding water if necessary. Garnish servings with shredded cheese.

Yield: 20 servings

HO-BO DINNERS

1 pound ground chuck
1 tablespoon Worcestershire sauce
1 tablespoon brown sugar
¼ teaspoon salt
¼ teaspoon pepper
1 onion, sliced
1 green bell pepper, sliced
4 potatoes, cut into strips
¼ cup Russian salad dressing

Combine ground chuck, Worcestershire sauce, brown sugar, salt and pepper in bowl; mix well. Shape into 4 patties; place on large square heavy-duty foil. Top each with onion, green pepper and potatoes. Add 1 tablespoon salad dressing to each. Fold and seal foil. Grill over hot coals for 1 hour or until potatoes are tender.

Yield: 4 servings

HOBO DINNER

1/4 pound lean ground beef
1 medium potato, peeled, chopped
1 carrot, peeled, sliced
1/2 onion, chopped
1 cup frozen mixed vegetables
Dash of salt and pepper

Crumble ground beef into center of 18-inch square heavy-duty foil. Layer potato, carrot, onion and frozen vegetables on top; mix gently. Season with salt and pepper. Seal foil, making double fold; roll up ends. Place on grill over hot coals. Cook for 1 hour or until vegetables are tender, turning every 15 minutes. Serve hot.

Yield: 1 serving

PRICKLY MEATBALLS

2 pounds ground beef
1 cup uncooked rice
1/2 cup chopped onion
1/3 cup water
1 teaspoon salt
Pepper to taste
1 (20-ounce) can tomatoes
3/4 cup water
3/4 teaspoon chili powder

Combine ground beef, rice, onion, 1/3 cup water, salt and pepper in bowl; mix well. Shape into small balls. Bring tomatoes, 3/4 cup water and chili powder to a boil in Dutch oven over medium coals. Add meatballs. Simmer, covered, for 1 hour, turning meatballs several times and basting with cooking liquid.

Yield: 8 servings

GROUND BEEF BUNDLES

1 pound ground beef
3 or 4 medium potatoes, thinly sliced
2 carrots, sliced
1 large onion, sliced
Salt, pepper and garlic powder to taste

Cut five 12×12-inch pieces of foil. Shape ground beef into patties. Place 1 on each foil sheet. Layer potatoes, carrots and onion over each patty, seasoning layers with salt, pepper and garlic powder. Seal foil. Place on hot coals. Cook for 30 minutes.

Yield: 5 servings

CAMPFIRE LASAGNA

2 pounds ground beef
1 (32-ounce) jar spaghetti sauce
1 spaghetti sauce jar water
1 (16-ounce) package lasagna noodles
8 ounces mozzarella cheese, shredded

Brown ground beef in Dutch oven over medium coals, stirring until crumbly; drain. Add spaghetti sauce and water; mix well. Cook until heated through, stirring occasionally. Add noodles; mix well. Simmer until noodles are tender, stirring frequently. Stir in cheese.

Yield: 8 servings

PIE IRON PIZZA

1 pound ground beef
1 (12-ounce) jar spaghetti sauce
1/4 cup butter, softened
20 slices bread

Brown ground beef in skillet, stirring until crumbly; drain. Stir in spaghetti sauce. Butter bread on 1 side. Place 2 slices bread buttered side out in each set of pie irons. Place meat sauce on 1 slice of bread; close irons. Place irons in coals. Cook for 5 to 10 minutes on each side, turning frequently to avoid burning.

Yield: 10 servings

PIZZA LOAVES

1 pound ground beef
½ cup chopped onion
1 (8-ounce) can pizza sauce
½ teaspoon each salt and oregano
¼ cup sliced stuffed olives
1 loaf French bread, split lengthwise
1 cup shredded Muenster cheese

Brown ground beef and onion in skillet, stirring frequently. Stir in pizza sauce, salt, oregano and olives. Place each bread half on foil. Spoon ground beef mixture over bread. Sprinkle with cheese. Seal foil. Cook over low coals for 15 minutes or until heated through.

Yield: 6 servings

GUMBOBURGERS

1 pound ground beef
1 small onion, chopped
1 can chicken gumbo soup
2 tablespoons catsup
2 tablespoons prepared mustard
Salt and pepper to taste
8 hamburger buns

Brown ground beef with onion in skillet, stirring until ground beef is crumbly; drain. Add next 5 ingredients. Simmer over low coals for 30 minutes. Serve on buns.

Yield: 8 servings

DUTCH OVEN STEW

4 pounds ground beef
4 cans vegetable soup
2 cups minute rice
1 small onion, chopped
1 (32-ounce) can tomato juice

Brown ground beef in Dutch oven over medium coals, stirring until crumbly. Add remaining ingredients; mix well. Simmer until rice is tender.

Yield: 15 servings

CORNY STEW

2 pounds ground beef
Salt and pepper to taste
1 onion, finely chopped
1 tablespoon vegetable oil
2 cans vegetable soup
1 (12-ounce) can whole kernel corn, drained

Combine ground beef, salt and pepper in bowl; mix well. Shape into small balls. Brown meatballs with onion in oil in Dutch oven over medium coals, stirring frequently; drain. Add soup and enough water to keep stew from sticking to Dutch oven. Cook, covered, over low heat until meatballs are cooked through. Stir in corn. Serve hot.

Yield: 8 servings

GREEN PEPPER BURGERS

1 pound ground beef
1 medium onion, minced
½ green bell pepper, minced
2 cloves of garlic, minced
2 teaspoons cumin
2 teaspoons coriander
1 teaspoon salt
¼ teaspoon pepper
3 large flour tortillas, cut into halves

Combine ground beef, onion, green pepper, garlic and seasonings in bowl; mix well. Shape into patties. Grill over hot coals until done to taste. Wrap each patty in flour tortilla half. Serve with fruit salad.

Yield: 6 servings

COLA HAM

1½ cups cubed ham
1 cup cola
2 (16-ounce) cans baked beans
2 tablespoons brown sugar
1 medium onion, minced

Soak ham in cola in bowl for 2 hours or longer. Combine ham, 1 cup liquid, beans, brown sugar and onion in 1-quart pan. Cook over low coals for 30 to 40 minutes.

Yield: 6 servings

HAM-CABBAGE BUNDLES

16 cabbage leaves
1 ham slice, cooked, chopped
1 (16-ounce) can green beans, drained
1 (16-ounce) can whole kernel corn, drained

Tear off eight 18-inch pieces of foil. Place 1 cabbage leaf on each piece of foil. Layer equal amounts of ham, beans and corn in each cabbage leaf. Top with another cabbage leaf. Seal foil securely. Place in hot coals. Cook for 5 to 10 minutes on each side or until heated through. Cabbage keeps meat and vegetables from burning. May substitute hot dogs, hamburger patties or beef stew for ham. May substitute potatoes or mixed vegetables for beans or corn if preferred.

Yield: 8 servings

OUTDOOR LORE

To make campfire baked apples, core apples, leaving ½ inch pulp in bottom. Fill with brown sugar. Add cinnamon, raisins, nuts, coconut, or dates to taste. Wrap in double thickness of foil. Place in hot coals. Cook for 10 minutes.

HAM KNAPSACKS

8 hamburger buns
¼ cup butter, softened
8 slices cooked ham
8 slices American cheese
8 slices pineapple

Spread cut sides of hamburger buns with butter. Layer ham, cheese and pineapple on bottoms of buns; cover with bun tops. Wrap individually in foil. Place on coals. Cook until heated through.

Yield: 8 servings

SPAMWICHES

1 (12-ounce) can Spam
3 hard-boiled eggs, chopped
2 cups shredded Cheddar cheese
¼ cup grated onion
1 can cream of mushroom soup
8 hamburger buns

Mash Spam with fork in bowl. Add eggs, cheese, onion and soup; mix well. Spread on buns; wrap in foil. Bake over hot coals for 15 minutes.

Yield: 8 servings

PORK BUNDLES

6 slices bacon, cut into halves
1 large Bermuda onion, sliced
6 pork tenderloin patties
1½ cups sliced carrots
1 large green bell pepper, cut into rings

Cut foil into six 12×12-inch pieces. Place 1 slice bacon in center of each square. Layer onion slice, pork tenderloin patty, carrot slices, green pepper ring and 1 slice bacon over each bacon slice. Seal foil securely. Cook over hot coals on grill for 20 minutes, turning frequently. Serve with applesauce, tossed green salad and fried potatoes.

Yield: 6 servings

GERMAN PORK CHOPS

½ cup butter
8 pork chops
1 (32-ounce) can sauerkraut, drained
1 (12-ounce) can non-alcoholic beer
1 cup sour cream
Salt and pepper to taste
2 or 3 large tart apples, cut into ¼-inch slices
⅓ to ½ cup packed brown sugar
Cinnamon to taste
Paprika to taste

Preheat 12-inch Dutch oven over 8 to 10 hot coals with 14 to 16 hot coals on top. Melt butter in oven. Add pork chops. Cook until brown. Remove pork chops. Add sauerkraut. Stir-fry for several minutes. Add non-alcoholic beer and sour cream; mix well. Remove half the sauerkraut mixture. Place 4 pork chops over remaining sauerkraut. Season with salt and pepper. Cover with half the apple slices. Sprinkle with half the brown sugar and cinnamon. Repeat layers. Sprinkle with paprika. Bake, covered with lid and coals, for 45 minutes or until pork chops are tender.

Yield: 6 to 8 servings

COUNTRY SHORT RIBS

Country-style short ribs
Meat tenderizer to taste
Salt and pepper to taste
Hickory chips, soaked in water
1 cup hickory-flavored barbecue sauce

Place ribs on foil. Sprinkle with meat tenderizer, salt and pepper. Fold foil to enclose ribs. Cook over hot coals for 1 hour. Place wet hickory chips over hot coals. Remove ribs from foil. Baste with barbecue sauce. Grill for 10 minutes, turning once.

Yield: variable

SAUSAGE STEW

1 turnip, peeled, cut into chunks
4 potatoes, peeled, cut into chunks
6 carrots, peeled, cut into chunks
2 pounds link sausage
8 peppercorns
1 head cabbage, cut into wedges

Place turnip, potatoes, carrots, sausage and peppercorns in cast-iron 12-inch Dutch oven. Add enough water to cover. Place on hanger over fire or directly on coals. Bring mixture to a boil. Cook for 30 minutes or until carrots are tender. Add cabbage. Cook for 15 minutes longer or until cabbage is tender.

Yield: 6 servings

BACON-WRAPPED DOGS

10 slices bacon
1 pound hot dogs
2 apples, sliced
4 slices American cheese, cut into strips

Cook bacon for 2 minutes on each side in skillet; drain. Cut slit lengthwise in each hot dog, not cutting completely through. Place 3 slices apple and 1 strip cheese in each hot dog. Wrap with bacon; secure with wooden picks. Grill 4 inches from medium coals for 12 to 15 minutes or to desired degree of doneness, turning frequently.

Yield: 10 servings

OUTDOOR LORE

Before using pans on wood or smoking fire, rub outside with brown soap for easier cleaning.

CHEESE DOG

1 hot dog
1 slice American cheese
1 slice bacon
1 hot dog bun

Cut lengthwise slit in hot dog. Fill with cheese. Wrap bacon around hot dog. Secure with wooden picks. Thread at an angle onto skewer or stick. Toast carefully, cheese side down, over hot coals. Rotate hot dog. Cook until bacon is crisp. Garnish as desired. Serve with hot dog bun.

Yield: 1 serving

CHILI DOGS IN A BLANKET

10 (6-inch) flour tortillas
10 hot dogs
1 (15-ounce) can chili with beans
1½ cups shredded American cheese
Sour cream to taste

Place each tortilla on sheet of heavy-duty foil. Place hot dog in center of each tortilla. Top each with 2 tablespoons chili and 2 tablespoons cheese. Roll to enclose filling; secure with wooden picks. Wrap tightly with foil. Place on grill 4 to 6 inches from hot coals. Grill for 10 to 15 minutes or until heated through. Serve with sour cream.

Yield: 10 servings

OUTDOOR LORE

Run 2 skewers through several hot dogs "ladder-fashion." You will be able to turn them all at once, and the hot dogs will stay on the grill.

FRANKWICHES

1 (10-count) package hot dogs, sliced
2 cups shredded mozzarella cheese
2 tablespoons prepared mustard
2 tablespoons pickle relish
1 tablespoon sugar
Catsup
12 to 16 hamburger buns

Combine hot dog slices, cheese, mustard and relish in bowl; mix well. Add sugar and enough catsup to coat hot dog slices well. Spoon into buns. Wrap individually in foil. Freeze if desired. Bake over hot coals for 30 minutes.

Yield: 12 to 16 servings

BEANY WEENY

3 (20-ounce) cans pork and beans
1 cup catsup
½ cup packed brown sugar
2 pounds hot dogs, sliced ½ inch thick

Combine pork and beans, catsup, brown sugar and hot dogs in Dutch oven; mix well. Cook over medium coals until heated through.

Yield: 12 servings

FRANK KABOBS

5 hot dogs
1 (16-ounce) can potatoes, drained
1 pint cherry tomatoes
1 (20-ounce) can pineapple chunks, drained
½ cup teriyaki sauce

Cut hot dogs into fourths. Thread hot dogs, potatoes, tomatoes and pineapple alternately onto skewers until all ingredients are used. Pour teriyaki sauce into small dish. Dip each skewer in sauce. Grill over hot coals until heated through, turning frequently.

Yield: 5 servings

HOBO MEAL

Ears of corn with silks
Whole potatoes
Small onions
Carrots
Cabbage, cut into quarters
Polish sausage
Ham, cut into thick slices (optional)
1 to 2 gallons water

Stand unhusked corn on end in large new metal trash can. Layer potatoes, onions, carrots, cabbage, sausage and ham over corn. Place 1 potato on top as tester. Pour in water. Cover tightly with lid or heavy foil. Punch 4 to 5 holes in top. Place on open fire. Cook until steam appears. Cook for 30 minutes or until test potato is tender.

Yield: variable

SUPER SKILLET SUPPER

1 (5½-ounce) package hashed brown potatoes
    with onion
1 (16-ounce) package cut green beans
1 (12-ounce) can luncheon meat, cut into
    strips
1½ cups water
1 (6-ounce) can evaporated milk
1 (5-ounce) jar cheese spread
¼ teaspoon hickory smoke
¼ teaspoon pepper

Combine potatoes, green beans, luncheon meat, water, evaporated milk, cheese spread, hickory smoke and pepper in heavy large skillet; cover. Cook over campfire or camp stove for 10 minutes or until mixture is bubbly and potatoes are tender, stirring occasionally. Garnish with additional luncheon meat strips.

Yield: 4 servings

BARBECUED CHICKEN

1 egg, beaten
1 cup vegetable oil
2 cups cider vinegar
3 tablespoons salt
1 tablespoon poultry seasoning
1 teaspoon pepper
10 chicken breasts

Combine egg, oil, vinegar, salt, poultry seasoning and pepper in bowl. Place chicken breasts in shallow dish. Pour marinade over chicken. Marinate, covered, in refrigerator for 45 minutes or longer. Drain, reserving marinade. Grill over hot coals for 1 hour or until chicken is tender, turning and basting with marinade every 10 minutes. The longer the chicken marinates, the better the flavor.

Yield: 10 servings

CHICKEN WITH MUSHROOMS

1 chicken, cut up
1 cup (about) flour
½ teaspoon salt
1 teaspoon garlic salt
1 cup (or more) vegetable oil for frying
1 (32-ounce) can tomato juice
1 (4-ounce) can mushrooms, drained

Coat chicken with flour; sprinkle with salt and garlic salt. Brown in 1 or more cups oil in Dutch oven over hot coals; drain. Add tomato juice and mushrooms; cover and return to coals. Arrange coals for simmering heat using Dutch oven directions. Simmer for 1 to 1½ hours or until chicken is tender.

Yield: 6 servings

CHICKEN AND STUFFING

8 skinless chicken breast halves
8 slices Swiss cheese
2 cans mushroom soup
1 cup sour cream
6 tablespoons chicken broth
2 packages cornmeal stuffing mix with
    herb seasonings
¼ cup chopped parsley
Melted butter

Preheat 12-inch Dutch oven over hot coals using 8 to 10 coals underneath and 12 to 14 coals on top. Place chicken breasts in oven. Place 1 slice cheese on each chicken breast. Combine soup, sour cream and chicken broth in bowl; mix well. Pour over chicken. Sprinkle stuffing mix and herb seasonings over top. Sprinkle with parsley. Drizzle with butter. Cover with lid and coals. Bake for 1 hour.

Yield: 8 servings

FLOWERPOT CHICKEN

Yogurt
Garlic, coriander, gingerroot, red pepper,
    cumin and salt to taste
Chicken, cut up
Whole wheat flour
Yeast

Combine yogurt and seasonings in bowl; mix well. Add chicken. Marinate, covered, in refrigerator for 6 hours or longer. Drain chicken. Line flowerpot with foil. Stand chicken pieces against side of pot. Place heatproof saucer on top. Place in medium coals. Cook until tender. Mix flour and yeast with enough water to form dough. Shape into 1½-inch balls; flatten to ¼-inch thickness. Place on saucer. Cook until brown on both sides. Repeat with remaining dough.

Yield: variable

FOILED CHICKEN

4 chicken thighs
4 chicken legs
1 onion, chopped
2 carrots, sliced
8 mushrooms, sliced
1 (16-ounce) can green beans, drained
1 can cream of celery soup

Cut four 12×16-inch pieces of foil. Place 2 pieces chicken on each piece of foil. Combine onion, carrots, mushrooms, green beans and celery soup in bowl; mix well. Spoon evenly over chicken. Fold foil to enclose. Grill over hot coals for 2 hours or until chicken is tender.

Yield: 4 servings

GRILLED CHICKEN

½ cup white grape juice
½ cup soy sauce
3 tablespoons grated fresh ginger
2 cloves of garlic, minced
4 chicken broiler halves
2 tablespoons olive oil

Combine white grape juice, soy sauce, ginger and garlic in bowl; mix well. Place chicken in shallow baking dish. Pour marinade over chicken. Marinate, covered, in refrigerator for several hours. Drain, reserving marinade. Place on grill over hot coals. Brush with olive oil. Broil for 10 to 12 minutes. Turn chicken; brush with olive oil. Broil for 10 minutes longer or until tender, basting with marinade if desired. May substitute ground ginger for fresh.

Yield: 4 servings

CHICKEN DINNER IN FOIL

2 chicken pieces
1 small potato, peeled
2 cherry tomatoes
1 small onion, peeled
2 mushroom caps
2 green bell pepper rings
2 tablespoons rice
1 tablespoon Worcestershire sauce
3/4 teaspoon salt
Dash each of pepper and paprika
1 teaspoon margarine

Place chicken, potato, tomatoes, onion, mushrooms, green pepper and rice on large piece of heavy-duty foil. Add seasonings and margarine. Seal foil tightly. Cook over hot coals for 1 1/4 hours or until chicken is tender, turning every 20 minutes.

Yield: 1 serving

OUTDOOR CHICKEN DIVAN

2 tablespoons salt
8 chicken breasts
2 cups rice
2 (10-ounce) packages frozen broccoli
2 cans cream of chicken soup
1 cup mayonnaise
2 teaspoons lemon juice
2 teaspoons (or more) curry powder

Fill Dutch oven 1/3 full of water. Add salt. Bring to a boil over medium coals. Add chicken. Cook, covered, for 20 minutes. Drain all but 4 cups water carefully. Add rice. Cook, covered, for 10 minutes, stirring occasionally. Add broccoli. Cook for 5 minutes. Combine soup, mayonnaise, lemon juice and curry powder in bowl; mix well. Spoon over chicken mixture. Simmer for 5 to 10 minutes or until heated through. Remove from coals. Let stand, covered, for 10 minutes.

Yield: 8 servings

SKILLET CHICKEN

4 pounds chicken pieces
1/2 cup flour
1/2 cup butter
2 cans cream of mushroom soup
1 soup can water

Coat chicken with flour. Brown on all sides in butter in 2 skillets over medium coals. Mix soup with water in bowl. Add half the mixture to each skillet. Simmer for 45 minutes or until tender. For Reflector Oven Chicken, arrange floured chicken in 2 buttered pans. Drizzle with butter. Bake in reflector oven for 40 minutes, turning once. Spread mixture of soup and water over chicken. Bake until tender.

Yield: 10 servings

ONION-BARBECUED CHICKEN

2 2/3 cups cooked rice
1 envelope dry onion soup mix
4 boned chicken breast halves
1/2 cup milk

Spray 4 large squares of foil with nonstick cooking spray. Place 2/3 cup rice on each. Layer 1 tablespoon soup mix, chicken, 1 tablespoon soup mix and 2 tablespoons milk on top of each. Seal foil securely. Place packets on grill over hot coals. Cook for 30 to 45 minutes; turn. Cook for 30 minutes longer or until chicken is tender.

Yield: 4 servings

OUTDOOR LORE

Premeasure and mix all dry ingredients for baking cakes, breads, etc. Place in airtight sealable plastic bag. Combine liquid ingredients in second bag. Pour into bag of dry ingredients to mix before baking on grill (see page 117).

"BATCHELOR" FLOUNDER

12 ounces flounder fillets
1 tablespoon tarragon
1 tablespoon basil
1/4 cup butter
1 tablespoon garlic powder
1 (4-ounce) can sliced mushrooms, drained

Shape foil into boat shape large enough to hold fish fillets. Spray with nonstick cooking spray. Place fillets in foil. Sprinkle with half the tarragon and basil. Melt butter in small saucepan. Stir in garlic powder. Drizzle half the butter mixture over fillets. Turn fillets. Sprinkle with remaining tarragon and basil; drizzle with remaining butter mixture. Grill 4 to 6 inches from hot coals for 5 minutes. Spoon mushrooms around sides of fillets. Grill until fish flakes easily. May substitute orange roughy or red snapper for flounder.

Yield: 2 servings

FOILED FISH

Large onion, sliced into rings
1/2 pound fish fillets per person
Butter
Parsley, chopped
Lemon slices
Salt and pepper to taste

Make foil pan of double-thick foil large enough to hold fish fillets in 1 layer. Pan sides should be 3 inches high. Layer half the onion rings, fish, dots of butter, parsley, lemon, remaining onion rings, salt and pepper on foil. Cover with foil; seal edges securely. Cook over hot coals for 10 minutes. Cut small hole in foil; check for doneness. Cook until fish flakes easily with fork.

Yield: variable

BROILED GROUPER STEAKS

1/3 cup butter
1/3 cup lemon juice
1/4 cup Worcestershire sauce
1/4 teaspoon onion salt
6 grouper steaks
Chopped parsley to taste

Melt butter in saucepan over hot coals. Add lemon juice, Worcestershire sauce and onion salt; mix well. Let stand until cool. Pour over fish steaks in shallow dish. Chill, covered, for 1 to 2 hours. Place fish in hinged wire grill, reserving marinade. Grill over hot coals for 6 to 8 minutes on each side or until fish flakes easily, basting with marinade occasionally. Sprinkle with parsley before serving.

Yield: 6 servings

PROVENÇAL SEA BASS

3 tablespoons olive oil
4 ounces mushrooms, thinly sliced
2 cloves of garlic, minced
Salt and pepper to taste
2 pounds sea bass fillets
2 tomatoes, chopped
1 green bell pepper, thinly sliced
8 ounces shrimp, peeled

Heat oil in skillet over hot coals. Add mushrooms. Sauté for 5 minutes. Add garlic, salt and pepper. Sauté for 5 minutes longer. Cut fish into 3×5-inch serving pieces. Place each fillet on foil square. Spoon mushroom mixture over fillets. Arrange tomatoes and green pepper over mushrooms. Top with shrimp. Seal foil. Cook on grill over medium coals for 15 to 20 minutes or until fish flakes easily. Drain filets; place on serving plate. Garnish with tomato wedges, olives, parsley sprigs and lemon wedges.

Yield: 4 to 6 servings

FOIL-BAKED FISH

Fish fillets
Onion slices
Lemon slices
Parsley, chopped
Salt and pepper to taste

Arrange fish fillets in single layer on large piece of heavy-duty foil. Top with onion slices and lemon slices. Sprinkle with parsley, salt and pepper. Seal foil tightly. Cook in medium coals for 15 minutes or until fish flakes easily.

Yield: variable

MONTANA FISH FRY

Fish fillets
Butter
Fresh lemon juice
Garlic salt to taste
Salt and pepper to taste

Arrange fish skin side down on sheet of foil. Place on grill over hot coals. Brush with mixture of equal parts butter and lemon juice seasoned with garlic salt, salt and pepper. Grill, uncovered, just until fish begins to flake; do not overcook. Remove from foil with spatula.

Yield: variable

HOT TUNAWICHES

4 (7-ounce) cans tuna, drained
1 stalk celery, finely chopped
1 pint mayonnaise-type salad dressing
1/4 cup finely chopped onion
25 hamburger buns
25 slices American cheese

Combine tuna, celery, salad dressing and onion in bowl; mix well. Spread on bottoms of buns. Top with cheese and bun tops. Wrap tightly in foil. Place in hot coals. Cook just until heated through.

Yield: 25 servings

HOT CREAMY TUNABURGERS

2 (6-ounce) cans tuna
1/4 cup green relish for hamburgers
1 can cream of chicken soup
1 can cream of mushroom soup
2 tablespoons minced green bell pepper
2 tablespoons minced onion
Dash of Tabasco sauce
Salt and pepper to taste
18 hamburger buns

Combine tuna, relish, soups, green pepper, onion and seasonings in bowl; mix well. Spoon between buns; wrap individually in foil. Bake over hot coals for 10 to 12 minutes.

Yield: 18 servings

BARBECUED SALMON

1 large salmon
2 teaspoons lemon juice
2 tablespoons butter, softened
Salt and pepper to taste

Rinse salmon and pat dry. Brush cavity with lemon juice. Rub with butter. Sprinkle with salt and pepper. Wrap tightly in foil, sealing well. Wrap with damp newspaper and second layer of foil. Place on grill over medium coals. Bake for 30 minutes on each side. Skin will stick to foil; salmon will be very moist.

Yield: 8 servings

SURPRISE SEAFOOD PACKETS

6 lobster tails
6 (2-ounce) haddock fillets
24 clams in shells
24 mussels in shells
1 cup butter
3 cloves of garlic, crushed
½ teaspoon tarragon
½ teaspoon rosemary
½ teaspoon thyme
¼ cup lemon juice
2 teaspoons salt
Freshly ground pepper to taste

Cut 6 large squares of heavy-duty foil. Cut through lobster tails with scissors. Layer 1 fish fillet, 1 lobster tail, 4 clams and 4 mussels on each square of foil. Combine butter, garlic, tarragon, rosemary, thyme, lemon juice, salt and pepper in saucepan. Heat until butter is melted, stirring to mix well. Drizzle over layers of seafood. Seal packets securely. Place on foil-lined grill. Grill for 15 to 20 minutes or until seafood is tender. Serve with Italian bread heated in foil on grill.

Yield: 6 servings

SHIPWRECK BREAKFAST

1 pound bacon
4 potatoes, boiled, cubed
8 eggs, beaten
Salt and pepper to taste
1 cup shredded Cheddar cheese

Cook bacon in skillet until crisp. Remove bacon to paper towels to drain; keep warm. Add cubed potatoes to bacon drippings. Sauté until brown, stirring to brown all sides; drain. Add eggs, salt and pepper. Scramble eggs until almost set. Add cheese and crumbled bacon. Cook eggs until done to taste.

Yield: 8 servings

BREAKFAST IN A BAG

12 slices bacon
12 eggs
Salt and pepper to taste

Place 1 slice of bacon flat in bottom of each of 12 paper bags. Break egg carefully on top of bacon in each bag. Season with salt and pepper. Gather top of each bag and tie securely to stick. Cook over hot coals for 15 minutes, taking care not to let bag burn.

Yield: 12 servings

CALIFORNIA EGG CRACKLE

1 pound bacon, chopped
12 eggs, beaten
½ cup milk
Salt and pepper to taste
¾ cup cheese cracker crumbs

Cook bacon in skillet until crisp; drain. Beat eggs, milk and seasonings in bowl. Add to hot skillet. Cook over hot coals until almost set, stirring constantly. Stir in cracker crumbs. Serve at once.

Yield: 9 servings

EGGS IN BOLOGNA

6 slices bologna
1 tablespoon vegetable oil
6 eggs
Salt and pepper to taste
1 tablespoon water

Brown bologna lightly on both sides in oil in skillet over medium coals. Bologna will curl up to form cups. Break 1 egg into each cup. Season with salt and pepper. Add 1 tablespoon water to skillet. Steam, covered, to desired degree of doneness. Serve on toast.

Yield: 6 servings

COWBOY'S BREAKFAST

8 slices bacon, cut into pieces
½ medium onion, chopped
2 potatoes, chopped
4 eggs
¼ cup milk

Fry bacon in skillet over medium coals until crisp. Drain partially, reserving drippings. Add onion to bacon in skillet. Sauté until onion is tender. Add potatoes; mix well. Cook, covered, until potatoes are tender, stirring frequently; add a small amount of reserved bacon drippings if necessary. Beat eggs and milk in mixer bowl until foamy. Pour over potatoes. Cook until eggs are set.

Yield: 4 servings

MILK CARTON EGGS

6 eggs

Fill six 1-quart waxed milk cartons halfway with water. Place 1 whole egg in each carton. Place in medium coals. Cook to desired degree of doneness. Remove from coals with tongs; drain. Milk carton will burn down to water level; egg shell will be discolored.

Yield: 6 servings

BEAN AND CELERY BAKE

2 cups water
3 (10-ounce) packages frozen green beans, thawed
3 cups 1-inch slices celery
3 tablespoons butter
½ teaspoon dillweed
Salt and pepper to taste

Bring water to a boil in Dutch oven over 8 hot coals. Stir in mixture of remaining ingredients. Cover with lid and 15 hot coals. Cook for 20 minutes or until vegetables are tender.

Yield: 10 servings

THREE-BEAN BAKE

1½ pounds ground beef
1 (16-ounce) can pork and beans
1 (20-ounce) can baby lima beans
1 (16-ounce) can kidney beans
¼ cup catsup
½ teaspoon salt
1 teaspoon dry mustard
1 tablespoon vinegar
1 tablespoon brown sugar
1 small onion, chopped

Brown ground beef in Dutch oven, stirring until crumbly; drain. Stir in pork and beans, lima beans, kidney beans, catsup, salt, dry mustard, vinegar, brown sugar and onion. Place in hot coals; cover. Top with hot coals. Cook for 30 minutes.

Yield: 12 servings

BEAN CASSEROLE

1 pound lean ground beef
1 onion, finely chopped
1 green bell pepper, finely chopped
2 (16-ounce) cans pork and beans
¼ cup packed brown sugar
1 tablespoon prepared mustard
¼ cup catsup
1 tablespoon steak sauce
1 teaspoon Worcestershire sauce
1 cup grated Cheddar cheese

Brown ground beef with onion and green pepper in skillet over hot coals, stirring frequently; drain. Stir in pork and beans, brown sugar, mustard, catsup, steak sauce and Worcestershire sauce. Simmer until heated through, stirring occasionally. Sprinkle with cheese. Serve when cheese melts.

Yield: 6 to 8 servings

BARBECUED CORN

4 ears of corn
4 teaspoons butter, softened
Salt and pepper to taste

Spread corn with butter; sprinkle with salt and pepper. Wrap tightly with foil. Place in hot coals. Cook until heated through, turning several times with tongs. Remove foil. Serve hot.

Yield: 4 servings

CORN IN HUSKS

6 or 8 ears of unhusked corn
¼ cup butter, softened
Salt and pepper to taste

Pull corn husks back; remove all corn silk. Reposition husks; tie with string. Soak in ice water to cover for 30 minutes to 2 hours. Place on grill over hot coals. Grill for 10 to 15 minutes or until husks are well-browned, turning several times. Remove husks. Serve with butter, salt and pepper.

Yield: 6 to 8 servings

FOIL-BAKED ONIONS

4 medium yellow onions
2 teaspoons margarine, softened

Peel onions. Cut into quarters to but not through bottom of onions. Place ½ teaspoon margarine into center of each cut onion. Wrap tightly in foil, twisting top of foil to seal. Place in hot coals. Cook until onions are transparent and tender. Onions will have a sweet taste almost like apples.

Yield: 4 servings

BACON-WRAPPED CABBAGE

1 head cabbage, cut into wedges
1 pound sliced bacon

Wrap each cabbage wedge with bacon slices. Place each wedge on foil square; seal foil. Place on grill over hot coals. Cook to desired degree of doneness.

Yield: 6 to 8 servings

CAMPFIRE FRENCH FRIES

1 medium potato, cut into strips
Seasoned salt and pepper to taste
1 tablespoon grated Parmesan cheese
1 tablespoon margarine
1 tablespoon bacon bits

Place potato on large square heavy-duty foil. Sprinkle with seasoned salt, pepper and cheese; toss to coat. Dot with margarine; sprinkle with bacon bits. Seal foil, leaving steam vent on top. Grill over hot coals for 30 to 45 minutes or until potato is tender, turning occasionally.

Yield: 1 serving

GRILLED POTATO WEDGES

4 medium potatoes, cut into wedges
1 green bell pepper, cut into strips
1 medium onion, sliced into thin rings
Pepper, celery salt or seasoned salt to taste
Margarine

Parboil potatoes for 5 minutes. Layer potatoes, green pepper strips and onion rings on 2 pieces of foil; sprinkle with seasonings. Dot with margarine. Seal foil. Place in hot coals under grill. Cook for 15 minutes or until green peppers are tender, turning once.

Yield: 4 servings

DUTCH OVEN POTATOES

10 large Irish potatoes
5 medium onions
12 ounces sliced bacon
¼ cup vegetable oil
Salt and pepper to taste
½ cup chicken broth
Paprika to taste

Peel and slice potatoes and onions. Chop bacon into small pieces. Brown bacon in Dutch oven over 10 hot coals. Add oil, potatoes and onions. Season with salt and pepper. Cover with lid and 15 hot coals. Cook for 15 minutes; turn potatoes. Cook for 5 minutes. Add chicken broth. Cook until brown, turning occasionally. Sprinkle with paprika. May add mushrooms, green or red bell peppers, pimento or Italian sausage if desired.

Yield: 10 servings

ZUCCHINI PARMESAN

½ cup grated Parmesan cheese
1 medium zucchini
½ cup chopped onion
Salt and pepper to taste

Spray large piece of foil with nonstick cooking spray. Sprinkle ¼ cup of Parmesan cheese onto foil. Peel zucchini. Slice into strips; place on cheese. Add onion. Sprinkle remaining Parmesan cheese, salt and pepper on top. Seal foil. Bake on grill over hot coals for 20 to 30 minutes or until zucchini is tender, turning packet once or twice.

Yield: 4 servings

GRILLED FRESH VEGETABLES

4 Japanese eggplant
4 zucchini or 2 zucchini and 2 yellow squash
3 tablespoons olive oil
1 to 2 cloves of garlic, minced

Cut vegetables into ¼-inch thick strips. Brush with oil. Sprinkle with garlic. Cook on grill over hot coals for 4 to 5 minutes or until tender, turning once. Serve with chicken, beef or fish.

Yield: 4 servings

FRYING PAN BREAD

1 cup flour
1 teaspoon baking powder
⅛ teaspoon salt
½ cup (about) water

Combine flour, baking powder and salt in bowl. Stir in enough water to make firm dough. Shape into large doughnut 1 inch thick. Make 2-inch hole in center. Place in preheated greased skillet. Cook over hot coals until brown on both sides. Serve immediately. May add 1 egg for richness, decreasing liquid; use milk instead of water; or add 1 tablespoon sugar for crisper crust.

Yield: 2 servings

CAMPER'S COFFEE CAKE

1 package blueberry muffin mix

Prepare muffin mix using package directions. Pour into 1 greased 9-inch foil pie pan. Invert 1 greased 9-inch foil pie pan over top; secure rims with spring-type clothespins. Place on grill 4 inches from hot coals. Cook for 15 minutes. Invert pans. Cook for 15 minutes longer.

Yield: 8 servings

MUFFINS IN ORANGE SHELLS

6 oranges
1 (7-ounce) package corn muffin mix
2 tablespoons butter

Cut off top ¼ of each orange, reserving tops. Remove and discard pulp to make hollow shells. Prepare muffin mix using package directions. Butter inside of orange shells lightly; do not butter lid. Pour enough muffin batter into shells to fill ½ full. Cover with orange lids. Wrap in foil. Bake on hot coals for 20 to 30 minutes. Remove foil.

Yield: 6 servings

CAMPFIRE CORN CAKES

2 cups cornmeal
1 tablespoon flour
2 tablespoons sugar
1 egg
¼ cup chopped onion
⅓ to ½ cup buttermilk

Combine first 5 ingredients with enough buttermilk to make medium batter in bowl; mix well. Drop by large spoonfuls onto preheated oiled cast-iron skillet. Cook over hot coals until brown on both sides, turning once. Place on paper towel. Serve in lined bread basket.

Yield: 8 or 9 servings

TONKA TOAST

Bread slices
Butter or margarine, softened
Toppings such as shredded Velveeta cheese, chopped onions, browned ground beef, spaghetti sauce, jam, mushrooms, peanut butter, fresh fruit

Spread 2 bread slices with butter. Place 1 slice in tonka iron. Add choice of toppings and 1 slice bread. Lock iron. Toast over hot coals.

Yield: variable

PEANUT PANCAKES

1¾ cups milk
1 egg
3 tablespoons peanut oil
1½ cups flour
2 tablespoons sugar
2 teaspoons baking powder
½ teaspoon salt
1¼ cups whole kernel corn
¼ cup chopped cocktail peanuts

Blend milk, egg and oil in bowl. Add flour, sugar, baking powder and salt. Beat with rotary beater until smooth. Stir in corn and peanuts. Pour 3 tablespoons at a time onto hot greased griddle. Bake over hot coals until brown on both sides.

Yield: 20 pancakes

YEAST PANCAKES

2 cups milk
2 eggs, beaten
2 tablespoons vegetable oil
2 tablespoons honey
3 tablespoons dry yeast
2 cups flour
1 teaspoon salt

Heat milk, eggs, oil and honey in saucepan over low coals until lukewarm. Sift yeast, flour and salt together into bowl. Add warm liquid ingredients; mix well. Let stand in warm place for 30 to 45 minutes or until light and foamy. Drop by spoonfuls onto hot greased griddle or skillet. Bake over hot coals until brown on both sides.

Yield: 6 servings

APPLES AND CRUMBLES

6 apples, cut up
½ cup sugar
2 tablespoons water
1½ cups biscuit mix
½ cup sugar
½ teaspoon cinnamon
1 egg, beaten
¼ cup melted butter

Preheat enough charcoal briquettes to cover top and bottom of Dutch oven, leaving 2 inches between coals. One briquette generates 40 degrees of heat. Place apples in greased 8-inch pan. Sprinkle with ½ cup sugar and water. Mix biscuit mix, ½ cup sugar and cinnamon in bowl. Add egg; stir with fork until crumbly. Spread over apples. Pour melted butter over top. Place in closed Dutch oven in coals; top with coals. Bake for 25 to 30 minutes or until apples are tender and crumbles are brown.

Yield: 6 servings

APPLESAUCE SPICE CAKE

1 (16-ounce) jar applesauce
1 (2-layer) package spice cake or gingerbread mix

Bring applesauce to a boil in cast-iron kettle over hot coals. Prepare cake batter using package directions. Pour over applesauce; cover. Bake over hot coals for 20 minutes or until cake tests done. Serve hot with whipped cream.

Yield: 15 servings

BANANAS FASTER

½ cup butter
1 cup packed brown sugar
8 ripe bananas
Cinnamon to taste
1 teaspoon rum extract

Melt butter in Dutch oven over medium-low coals. Stir in brown sugar. Cut bananas lengthwise into thin slices. Add to brown sugar mixture. Cook until tender. Sprinkle with cinnamon. Add rum extract. Cook until bubbly. Serve immediately.

Yield: 8 servings

FRUIT DUMPLINGS

1 (21-ounce) can pie filling
½ cup water
1 egg
2 tablespoons vegetable oil
¼ cup sugar
¼ cup milk
1 cup pancake mix

Bring mixture of pie filling and water to a boil in saucepan over hot coals. Combine egg, oil, sugar, milk and pancake mix in bowl; mix well. Drop by spoonfuls into hot mixture. Cook, covered, for 10 minutes.

Yield: 6 servings

PEACH DELIGHT

4 peaches, cut into halves
½ cup packed brown sugar
½ cup chopped pecans

Place each peach half on square of foil. Sprinkle with brown sugar and pecans. Seal foil tightly. Place in hot coals. Cook for 10 minutes. May use canned peaches if desired.

Yield: 8 servings

CAMP PEACH COBBLER

2 (30-ounce) cans sliced peaches
1 cup sugar
¼ cup flour
¼ cup butter
2 cups baking mix
½ cup milk
½ cup sugar
1 egg
1 teaspoon cinnamon
¼ cup sugar

Pour peaches into stockpot, reserving cans. Combine 1 cup sugar and flour in 1 empty peach can. Cut in butter until crumbly. Stir into peaches. Bring to a boil, covered, over hot coals. Mix baking mix, milk, ½ cup sugar and egg in remaining peach can until smooth. Drop by teaspoonfuls into boiling peach mixture. Sprinkle with mixture of cinnamon and ¼ cup sugar. Cover with lid. Place hot coals on lid. Cook over slow coals for 15 minutes or until dumplings are cooked through. Serve immediately with homemade ice cream or half-and-half.

Yield: 12 servings

PIE IRON DESSERT

1 tablespoon margarine, softened
2 slices bread
2 tablespoons cherry pie filling

Spread margarine on 1 side of bread. Place buttered side out in pie iron. Spread pie filling on 1 slice bread. Close pie iron; remove excess bread from edges. Place in medium coals. Cook for 5 minutes on each side or until golden brown. May substitute other pie filling for cherry or fill with peanut butter and chocolate chips if desired.

Yield: 1 serving

PINEAPPLE CAKE

1 cup butter
1 cup packed brown sugar
9 slices pineapple, drained
9 maraschino cherries
1 (8-ounce) can crushed pineapple
1½ packages yellow cake mix
½ cup sugar
1 tablespoon cornstarch
1 cup water
2 tablespoons butter
½ teaspoon grated lemon rind
1½ tablespoons lemon juice

Line Dutch oven with foil, leaving edges so cake can be lifted out and inverted. Melt 1 cup butter in Dutch oven over 8 hot coals. Stir in brown sugar. Arrange pineapple slices over brown sugar mixture. Place cherry in center of each slice. Spoon crushed pineapple around pineapple slices. Prepare cake mix using package directions. Pour over pineapple. Cover with lid and 14 hot coals. Bake for 30 to 35 minutes or until cake is golden brown and tests done, checking after 15 minutes. Lift cake out; invert onto serving plate. Combine sugar and cornstarch in saucepan. Stir in water. Cook until thickened, stirring constantly. Remove from heat. Stir in 2 tablespoons butter, lemon rind and juice. Serve with cake.

Yield: 15 to 20 servings

SHAGGY DOGS

2 cups chocolate chips
1 (14-ounce) can flaked coconut
1 (16-ounce) package marshmallows

Place chocolate chips in foil package. Place near campfire until melted. Spread flaked coconut on plate. Place marshmallow on fork; dip in chocolate and roll in coconut.

Yield: 40 servings

Great Grilling

If there's one experience most Americans have in common, other than taxes, it may well be the backyard barbecue. Nearly 80 percent of all the families in the United States own a grill—some 63 million households. Regardless of where you live, whether it's in a large suburban home or a small apartment, you've probably got some kind of outdoor grill, and in this chapter you'll find great new ways to use it.

For starters, our *Weekend Brunch* is a unique way to celebrate the day off, with such breakfast standbys as eggs and bacon used in innovative recipes. Fight burger burnout with an up-to-date new *Burger Bonanza*, complete with low-fat turkey burgers and a stuffing burger—pure Americana, with a twist.

You say all you've got is a four-by-eight balcony and a hibachi to work with? Our *Balcony Barbecue* is made to order for less-is-more gourmet. And continuing the "less" theme, try our new low-cal, low-fat *Lighten Up Barbecue* recipes, and our *Grilled Garden Supper*'s grilled veggies and fresh peach cobbler.

You might keep in mind that 60 percent of the backyard barbecuing in this country is done by men, most of whom could use some new recipes. Give this cookbook to a deserving fellow.

3

WEEKEND BRUNCH

Tuna Mold Appetizer with Crackers

Yummy Mac Salad

Beef and Bacon Twirls

Italian Cheese Ring

Chinese Chicken Wings

Nutty Apple Crisp   **Orange Julius**

The aroma of this brunch cooking—on the grill and in the oven—will wake up the sleepiest heads. The traditional bacon and eggs are found in the entrée and salad. Eat outdoors for a great start to the weekend.

TUNA MOLD APPETIZER

1½ envelopes unflavored gelatin
½ cup cold water
1 can tomato soup
8 ounces cream cheese, softened
2 (6-ounce) cans water-pack tuna
1 cup mayonnaise
1 cup each chopped celery and green onions
1½ teaspoons Worcestershire sauce
Tabasco sauce to taste

Soften gelatin in cold water. Heat soup and cream cheese in saucepan until smooth and creamy, stirring constantly. Add gelatin. Heat until gelatin dissolves completely. Add tuna, mayonnaise, celery, green onions and seasonings; mix well. Pour into 1½-quart mold greased with mayonnaise. Chill until firm. Unmold onto serving plate. Serve with crackers.

Yield: 15 servings

YUMMY MAC SALAD

2 cups uncooked macaroni
6 hard-boiled eggs, chopped
1 cup shredded Cheddar cheese
2 tomatoes, chopped
1 cup mayonnaise-type salad dressing
½ cup French salad dressing
3 tablespoons sugar

Cook pasta using package directions; drain and cool. Combine with eggs, cheese and tomatoes in salad bowl. Blend salad dressings and sugar in small bowl. Add to pasta mixture; mix gently. Chill until serving time.

Yield: 6 to 8 servings

BEEF AND BACON TWIRLS

1½ pounds well-trimmed round steak
Meat tenderizer
8 ounces sliced bacon
¼ to ½ teaspoon garlic powder
Salt and pepper to taste
2 tablespoons minced fresh parsley

Pound steak to ½-inch thickness or thinner. Sprinkle with meat tenderizer using package directions. Let stand for several minutes. Fry bacon until cooked through but not crisp. Sprinkle steak with garlic powder, salt, pepper and parsley. Place bacon strips lengthwise on steak; roll as for jelly roll from narrow end. Secure with wooden picks at 1-inch intervals. Cut into 1-inch slices between wooden picks. Grill over hot coals for 8 to 10 minutes, turning once. Place on serving plate; remove wooden picks.

Yield: 6 servings

ITALIAN CHEESE RING

2 tablespoons sesame seed
2½ cups flour
¼ cup sugar
1½ teaspoons salt
2 envelopes dry yeast
1 cup each water and milk
½ cup margarine
2 eggs
2 to 3 cups flour
1 cup shredded mozzarella cheese
½ teaspoon Italian seasoning
¼ teaspoon garlic powder
¼ cup margarine, softened

Grease 12-cup fluted tube pan generously; sprinkle with sesame seed. Combine 2½ cups flour, sugar, salt and yeast in mixer bowl. Heat water, milk and ½ cup margarine in saucepan to 120 to 130 degrees. Add milk mixture and eggs to flour mixture. Beat at low speed until moistened. Beat at medium speed for 3 minutes. Stir in enough remaining flour to make stiff batter. Combine cheese, Italian seasoning, garlic powder and ¼ cup margarine in bowl; mix well. Spoon half the batter into prepared tube pan. Spread cheese mixture over batter to within ½ inch of side of pan. Top with remaining batter. Let rise, covered, in warm place for 30 minutes or until doubled in bulk. Bake at 350 degrees for 30 to 40 minutes or until golden brown. Invert onto wire rack.

Yield: 24 servings

CHINESE CHICKEN WINGS

3 pounds chicken wings
2 tablespoons vegetable oil
1 cup honey
½ cup soy sauce
2 tablespoons catsup
1 clove of garlic, crushed

Remove and discard wing tips; disjoint wings. Place wings in shallow dish. Brush with oil. Combine remaining ingredients in bowl; mix well.

Pour over wings. Marinate, covered, in the refrigerator for 2 hours. Arrange wings on grill 4 to 5 inches above medium coals. Cook for 10 minutes on each side.

Yield: 2½ dozen

NUTTY APPLE CRISP

6 cups sliced peeled apples
¼ cup raisins
2 tablespoons sugar
½ cup rolled oats
½ cup packed brown sugar
¼ cup flour
½ teaspoon cinnamon
¼ cup margarine
½ cup chopped nuts

Combine apples, raisins and sugar in bowl; toss lightly to mix. Place in ungreased 9-inch square baking pan. Combine oats, brown sugar, flour and cinnamon in small bowl. Cut in margarine until crumbly. Mix in nuts. Sprinkle over apple mixture. Bake at 375 degrees for 30 minutes or until apples are tender and topping is brown.

Yield: 6 to 8 servings

ORANGE JULIUS

1 (6-ounce) can frozen orange juice
    concentrate, thawed
1 cup milk
1 cup water
½ cup sugar
1 teaspoon vanilla extract
10 to 12 ice cubes

Combine all ingredients in blender container. Process until ice is crushed and mixture is frothy. Serve in juice glasses as appetizer or in larger glasses if desired.

Yield: 4 to 8 servings

BURGER BONANZA

Broccoli-Cauliflower Salad

Sausage and Cheese Dip

Bevy of Burgers

Sour Cream Potatoes

Baked Beans

Best-Ever Brownies

Nothing beats the All-American hamburger for a cookout. We've paired our unusual trio with other favorites for a menu sure to please everyone in your family.

BROCCOLI-CAULIFLOWER SALAD

1 bunch broccoli
1 head cauliflower
1 medium red onion
1 large green bell pepper
1 bunch green onions
1 medium package radishes
¼ head red cabbage
¾ cup mayonnaise
⅓ cup wine vinegar
⅓ cup vegetable oil
¼ cup sugar

Chop all vegetables coarsely; combine in bowl. Blend mayonnaise, vinegar, oil and sugar in small bowl. Add to vegetables; mix well. Chill, covered, for 30 minutes.

Yield: 8 to 10 servings

SAUSAGE AND CHEESE DIP

1 pound hot sausage
1 pound Velveeta cheese, chopped
1 (16-ounce) can chili without beans

Brown sausage in skillet, stirring until crumbly; drain. Combine cheese and chili in 3-quart saucepan. Heat until cheese melts, stirring constantly. Stir in sausage. Serve warm with corn chips or crackers.

Yield: 20 servings

GRILLED TURKEY BURGERS

2 pounds ground fresh turkey
1 egg, lightly beaten
½ cup seasoned croutons, crushed
¼ cup instant minced onion
2 tablespoons Worcestershire sauce

Combine all ingredients in bowl; mix well. Divide into 8 portions; shape into patties. Grill over hot coals to desired degree of doneness.

Yield: 8 servings

STUFFINBURGERS

1 cup herb-seasoned stuffing mix
¾ cup milk
1 teaspoon instant minced onion
1 pound ground beef
1 teaspoon salt
½ teaspoon MSG
¼ teaspoon pepper
4 or 5 hamburger buns
4 or 5 slices each onion and tomato

Combine stuffing mix, milk and onion in bowl. Let stand until moistened. Add ground beef and seasonings; mix well. Shape into 4 or 5 patties. Broil over hot coals for 7 to 8 minutes; turn patties over. Broil to taste. Place patties on hamburger buns. Top with onion and tomato slices.

Yield: 4 or 5 servings

TORPEDO BURGER

2 pounds lean ground beef
1 (8-ounce) can crushed pineapple
⅓ cup chopped green onions
3 tablespoons soy sauce
1 teaspoon garlic powder
1 long loaf French bread
3 tablespoons melted butter
Salt to taste
1 green bell pepper, sliced into rings
1 tomato, sliced

Combine first 5 ingredients in bowl; mix well. Shape to resemble French bread in size. Preheat gas grill on High for 10 minutes. Place ground beef loaf on grill; reduce temperature to Medium and close cover. Grill for 10 minutes. Turn loaf over. Grill for 10 minutes longer. Slice bread into halves lengthwise. Brush cut sides with butter. Place buttered sides down on warming rack of grill. Heat until golden brown. Place ground beef loaf on bottom half of bread. Season to taste. Top with green pepper, tomato slices and top of bread. Cut into serving portions.

Yield: 4 to 6 servings

SOUR CREAM POTATOES

2 tablespoons margarine, softened
1 cup sour cream
1 envelope dry onion soup mix
¼ cup light cream
1 (9- to 12-ounce) package frozen French-fried
   potatoes, thawed

Combine margarine, sour cream, soup mix and cream in bowl; mix well. Add potatoes; stir gently to coat. Pour into greased 8-inch baking pan. Bake in closed preheated grill on Medium for 25 to 30 minutes.

Yield: 4 servings

BAKED BEANS

1 (42-ounce) can pork and beans
½ cup chopped onion
½ cup chopped green bell pepper
½ cup catsup
⅓ cup molasses
2 tablespoons brown sugar
2 tablespoons prepared mustard
2 teaspoons chili powder
⅛ teaspoon garlic powder
3 slices crisp-fried bacon, crumbled

Combine first 9 ingredients in bowl; mix well. Spoon into lightly greased shallow 2-quart baking dish. Bake at 350 degrees for 55 minutes. Top with bacon. Bake for 5 minutes longer.

Yield: 8 servings

BEST-EVER BROWNIES

2 cups sugar
1½ cups flour
10 tablespoons baking cocoa
1 cup vegetable oil
4 eggs
2 teaspoons vanilla extract
1 cup chopped walnuts
½ cup corn oil margarine
¼ cup baking cocoa
6 tablespoons milk
4⅓ cups confectioners' sugar

Combine first 3 ingredients in bowl; mix well. Add oil, eggs and vanilla; mix with wooden spoon until smooth. Stir in walnuts. Pour into ungreased 9x13-inch baking pan. Bake at 350 degrees for 30 minutes. Bring margarine, ¼ cup cocoa and milk to a boil in heavy saucepan, stirring frequently; remove from heat. Pour into mixer bowl. Add confectioners' sugar. Beat at medium speed until creamy. Pour over hot brownies. Let stand until cool. Cut into squares.

Yield: 5 dozen

BALCONY BARBECUE

Queso with Chips or
Cheese Balls with Olives

Marinated Veggies

Macaroni Ring Salad

Boneless Chicken Breasts

Onioned Potatoes

In-a-Jiffy Cake or
Chocolate Almond Pie

Cooking out doesn't require all of the great outdoors—just your little piece of it. And the balcony is a perfect place for a small grill or hibachi. Salads and desserts kept in the refrigerator are only a few steps away.

QUESO

12 ounces ground beef
8 ounces sausage
½ onion, chopped
1 (10-ounce) can Ro-Tel tomatoes
1 pound Velveeta cheese, chopped

Cook ground beef, sausage and onion in large skillet, stirring until ground beef is crumbly; drain. Heat Ro-Tel tomatoes and Velveeta cheese in saucepan until cheese melts, stirring frequently. Add ground beef mixture; mix well. Serve warm with favorite chips.

Yield: 20 servings

CHEESE BALLS WITH OLIVES

1 cup flour
2 cups shredded Cheddar cheese
½ cup butter
Dash of Worcestershire sauce
1 jar small stuffed olives

Combine flour and cheese in bowl. Cut in butter until crumbly. Add Worcestershire sauce. Mix with hands until mixture forms dough. Pinch off small portions of dough; shape around olives, covering completely. Place on baking sheet. Bake at 425 degrees for 12 minutes or until light brown.

Yield: 1 to 2 dozen

MARINATED VEGGIES

1 (6-ounce) can vegetable juice cocktail
¼ cup vegetable oil
2 tablespoons vinegar
1 envelope Italian salad dressing mix
2 cups cauliflowerets
1 cup sliced carrots
1 cup chopped zucchini
½ cup green bell pepper squares

Combine vegetable juice cocktail, oil, vinegar and salad dressing mix in jar; shake to mix. Combine vegetables in bowl; pour marinade over top. Marinate, covered, in refrigerator for 4 hours or longer, stirring occasionally.

Yield: 8 servings

OUTDOOR LORE

To bake potatoes in half the usual time, let potatoes stand in boiling water to cover for 15 minutes before baking on grill.

To turn your grill into an oven, place triple thickness of foil shiny side up on grill rack, leaving 2 inches all around for heat circulation. Bake cakes, breads or pies as usual.

MACARONI RING SALAD

1 package macaroni rings
4 ounces Velveeta cheese, shredded
1 cucumber, peeled, chopped
2 tomatoes, chopped
Salt and pepper to taste
3/4 cup sour cream
1 cup mayonnaise-type salad dressing
1/2 cup sandwich spread
1 onion, chopped
1/2 cup sugar
1/4 cup prepared mustard

Cook macaroni rings using package directions. Combine with cheese, cucumber, tomatoes, salt and pepper in bowl. Combine sour cream, salad dressing, sandwich spread, onion, sugar and mustard in bowl; mix well. Pour over macaroni mixture; mix gently until coated.

Yield: 8 to 10 servings

BONELESS CHICKEN BREASTS

4 boneless chicken breasts
1/4 cup Worcestershire sauce
2 tablespoons lemon juice
1/4 cup margarine
1/2 teaspoon salt
Pepper to taste

Place chicken on preheated grill. Cook on 1 side until brown. Blend Worcestershire sauce and remaining ingredients in small saucepan. Heat on grill. Brush over chicken. Cook chicken until tender, turning and basting frequently.

Yield: 4 servings

ONIONED POTATOES

6 medium baking potatoes
1/2 cup butter, softened
1 envelope dry onion soup mix

Scrub potatoes; do not peel. Cut each into 3 or 4 slices lengthwise. Spread with mixture of butter and soup mix. Reassemble potatoes and wrap each in heavy-duty foil, sealing tightly. Place on grill over low coals. Cook for 45 minutes to 1 hour or until tender, turning occasionally.

Yield: 6 servings

IN-A-JIFFY CAKE

1 1/2 cups sifted cake flour
3/4 cup sugar
1/4 teaspoon salt
2 teaspoons baking powder
3/4 cup milk
1 teaspoon vanilla extract
1/4 cup melted shortening
1 egg, beaten

Sift dry ingredients together 3 times; place in mixer bowl. Combine milk, vanilla, shortening and egg in bowl; mix well. Add to dry ingredients. Beat for 2 minutes. Pour into greased 8-inch square cake pan. Bake at 350 degrees for 30 minutes.

Yield: 8 servings

CHOCOLATE ALMOND PIE

2 envelopes whipped topping mix
2 small packages sugar-free chocolate instant
    pudding mix
3 cups skim milk
2 tablespoons almond extract
1 baked (9-inch) pie shell
8 ounces whipped topping

Prepare whipped topping mix using package directions. Combine with pudding mix, milk and almond extract in large bowl; mix until well blended. Pour into pie shell. Top with whipped topping. Garnish with almonds or chocolate curls or shavings.

Yield: 8 servings

BACKYARD POTLUCK DINNER

Old-Fashioned Cheese Ball

Secret Crab Spread

Medley of Salads

Hot Dogs with Brunswick Chili

Chicken Cacciatore

Barbecued Beans

Sour Cream Potatoes

Grilled French Bread

Poppy Seed Cake

Lemonade Pies

Have family or friends over the easy way. Everyone brings a favorite dish, while you grill the bread and potatoes. Enjoy the cool of the evening without heating up the kitchen.

OLD-FASHIONED CHEESE BALL

4 ounces bleu cheese, softened
4 ounces smoky cheese spread, softened
8 ounces Old English cheese, softened
6 ounces cream cheese, softened
1 tablespoon parsley flakes
1 tablespoon onion flakes
1 cup finely chopped pecans

Combine first 6 ingredients in mixer bowl; beat until blended. Shape into ball; roll in pecans. Chill until firm. Serve with crackers.

Yield: 6 servings

SECRET CRAB SPREAD

16 ounces cream cheese, softened
1 package imitation crab meat
1 to 2 cups cocktail sauce
Catsup and prepared horseradish to taste

Layer cream cheese and crab meat on serving plate. Spread mixture of remaining ingredients over top. Serve with Triscuits.

Yield: 10 servings

OLD-FASHIONED FRUIT SALAD

1 small can mandarin oranges, drained
2 apples, chopped
1 small can pineapple chunks, drained
1 large can fruit cocktail, drained
2 bananas, sliced
2 tablespoons lemon juice
½ cup chopped pecans
½ cup shredded coconut

Mix first 4 ingredients in bowl. Chill until serving time. Dip bananas into lemon juice. Add bananas, pecans and coconut to fruit mixture; mix well.

Yield: 6 to 8 servings

OKLAHOMA CABBAGE SLAW

1 large head cabbage, shredded
1 large purple onion, shredded
14 tablespoons sugar
1 cup white vinegar
¾ cup vegetable oil
1 tablespoon each salt and dry mustard
2 tablespoons sugar
1 teaspoon celery seed

Layer first 3 ingredients in large bowl; do not stir. Bring remaining ingredients to a boil in saucepan. Pour over cabbage mixture; do not stir. Cover immediately. Chill for 4 hours or longer. Store in refrigerator for 1 week or longer.

Yield: 10 to 12 servings

CONGEALED VEGETABLE SALAD

2 (6-ounce) packages lime gelatin
3 cups boiling water
2 cups shredded cheese
1¾ cups chopped celery
½ cup chopped pimento
2 medium onions, finely chopped
2 green bell peppers, finely chopped
2 cups grated cabbage
2 cups mayonnaise
1½ tablespoons sugar
1 tablespoon salt
3½ tablespoons vinegar
¾ cup chopped nuts

Dissolve gelatin in boiling water in large bowl. Let stand until cooled. Add remaining ingredients; mix well. Chill until firm.

Yield: 20 servings

CRUNCHY VEGETABLE SALAD

1 cup vegetable oil
1 cup sugar
½ cup vinegar
1 (16-ounce) can cut green beans, drained
1 (16-ounce) can green peas, drained
1 can sliced water chestnuts, drained
4 large stalks celery, finely chopped
1 (4-ounce) can chopped pimento
Salt to taste

Combine oil, sugar and vinegar in bowl; stir until sugar dissolves. Add vegetables and salt; mix well. Marinate, covered, in refrigerator for 8 hours to overnight. May add mushrooms or cocktail onions. Drain. Serve as vegetable or on lettuce as salad.

Yield: 8 servings

BRUNSWICK CHILI

3 pounds lean ground beef
2 tablespoons paprika
2½ tablespoons chili powder
1½ teaspoons crushed red pepper
1 tablespoon salt
1 tablespoon celery salt
Several cloves of garlic, chopped
1 tablespoon black pepper
2 small cans tomato sauce
1 cup water

Brown ground beef in Dutch oven, stirring frequently until crumbly; drain. Add remaining ingredients; mix well. Simmer for 3 hours. Use as hot dog chili.

Yield: 24 servings

CHICKEN CACCIATORE

6 chicken breasts, skinned
¼ cup margarine
1 cup sliced green onions
½ cup chopped green bell pepper
1 clove of garlic, crushed
½ teaspoon oregano leaves
½ teaspoon basil leaves
¼ teaspoon pepper
¼ teaspoon celery seed
1 bay leaf
1 (16-ounce) can low-sodium tomatoes
2 tablespoons flour

Brown chicken in margarine in skillet; remove chicken. Add green onions, green pepper and garlic. Sauté until tender. Add seasonings and tomatoes. Add chicken. Simmer, covered, for 1 hour, turning chicken once. Remove chicken to serving platter; discard bay leaf. Blend flour with a small amount of pan juices. Stir into skillet. Cook for 3 minutes or until thickened, stirring constantly. Pour over chicken. Garnish with parsley.

Yield: 6 servings

BARBECUED BEANS

1 pound ground beef
½ cup chopped onion
1 (38-ounce) can pork and beans
½ cup catsup
1 tablespoon Worcestershire sauce
1 teaspoon prepared mustard
¼ cup packed brown sugar
4 slices bacon

Cook ground beef with onion in skillet, stirring until ground beef is crumbly; drain. Add pork and beans, catsup, Worcestershire sauce, prepared mustard and brown sugar; mix well. Spoon into 2-quart casserole. Top with bacon. Bake at 350 degrees for 30 minutes.

Yield: 6 to 8 servings

SOUR CREAM POTATOES

4 cups chopped peeled potatoes
Salt to taste
6 green onions, chopped
2 (1.25-ounce) packages sour cream
  sauce mix
1 cup milk
Salt and pepper to taste
8 ounces Velveeta cheese, sliced

Cook potatoes in salted water to cover until tender; drain. Add green onions. Blend sauce mix with milk and salt and pepper in small bowl. Add to potatoes; mix well. Spoon into baking dish. Top with cheese; cover with foil. Place on side of grill; turn other side of grill on Medium. Cook for 30 minutes.

Yield: 6 servings

GRILLED FRENCH BREAD

1 long loaf French bread
½ cup butter, softened
1 clove of garlic, crushed
⅓ cup Parmesan cheese

Slice loaf into halves lengthwise. Mix butter and garlic. Spread garlic butter over cut sides of bread; sprinkle with cheese. Place cut sides together. Wrap loaf in heavy-duty foil. Place on grill 5 inches above medium coals. Heat for 15 minutes, turning occasionally.

Yield: 4 to 6 servings

POPPY SEED CAKE

2 tablespoons (about) sugar
1 (2-layer) package golden butter cake mix
½ cup sugar
¼ cup poppy seed
¾ cup vegetable oil
1 cup sour cream
4 eggs

Grease bundt pan with oil; sprinkle with 2 tablespoons sugar. Combine cake mix, ½ cup sugar, poppy seed, oil and sour cream in mixer bowl; beat until well blended. Add eggs 1 at a time, beating for 30 seconds after each addition. Pour into prepared pan. Bake at 350 degrees for 1 hour.

Yield: 16 servings

LEMONADE PIES

16 ounces whipped topping
1 (6-ounce) can frozen lemonade concentrate,
  thawed
1 (15-ounce) can sweetened condensed milk
2 graham cracker pie shells

Combine first 3 ingredients in mixer bowl; beat until blended. Pour into pie shells. Chill, covered, until serving time.

Yield: 12 to 16 servings

GRILLED GARDEN SUPPER

Peppery Barbecued Ribs

Marinated Copper Carrots

Peach Cobbler

Fresh from the garden to the table, the ingredients for this supper can be as close as your own backyard or the nearest vegetable stand. Although everything can be made or started ahead, begin with the freshest ingredients for a truly memorable feast.

PEPPERY BARBECUED RIBS

4 pounds spareribs, cut into 2-rib pieces
2 teaspoons onion powder
1 teaspoon red pepper
Salt to taste
1/8 teaspoon black pepper
1/2 teaspoon garlic powder
4 teaspoons Worcestershire sauce
2 cups water
1/3 cup sugar
1 cup lemon juice

Place spareribs on rack in shallow roasting pan. Bake at 400 degrees for 30 minutes, turning once; drain. Combine seasonings and water in saucepan. Bring to a boil; reduce heat. Simmer, covered, for 5 minutes; remove from heat. Stir in sugar and lemon juice. Place ribs on grill 4 inches above hot coals. Brush with half the sauce. Grill for 10 minutes. Turn ribs over. Brush with remaining sauce. Grill for 10 minutes longer or until glazed and cooked through.

Yield: 4 servings

MARINATED COPPER CARROTS

2 pounds carrots, sliced into rounds
1 onion, sliced into rounds
1 green bell pepper, cut into strips
1 can tomato soup or 1 cup tomato sauce
1 cup sugar
1/2 cup vegetable oil
3/4 cup white vinegar
1 teaspoon salt (optional)
1 tablespoon prepared mustard or 1 teaspoon
  dry mustard
1 teaspoon to 1 tablespoon Worcestershire
  sauce
Salt and pepper to taste

Cook carrots in a small amount of water in saucepan until tender-crisp; drain and rinse with cold water. Layer vegetables in bowl. Bring remaining ingredients to a boil in saucepan; pour over vegetables. Marinate, covered, in refrigerator for 24 hours, stirring occasionally.

Yield: 8 to 10 servings

PEACH COBBLER

5 or 6 peaches, peeled, sliced
1/2 cup sugar
1/2 teaspoon each cinnamon and nutmeg
1 stick margarine, sliced
1/2 cup water
4 1/2 teaspoons (rounded) shortening
1 cup flour
1/2 teaspoon salt

Layer first 5 ingredients in buttered 9x13-inch baking dish. Drizzle water over top. Cut shortening into mixture of flour and salt in small bowl until crumbly. Roll on lightly floured surface; cut into strips. Arrange strips lattice-fashion over peach mixture. Bake at 350 degrees for 30 minutes or until golden brown.

Yield: 8 servings

LIGHTEN UP BARBECUE

Piña Colada Fruit Dip with Fresh Fruit Dippers

Low-Cal Vegetable Salad or Barbecue Slaw

Dashed Potatoes

Teriyaki Pinwheels

Low-Cal Chicken

Banana Frozen Yogurt

We've trimmed the extra calories from this delicious dinner so you can have your barbecue and eat it too. For even lighter fare, you can omit the oil from the salad and main dish.

PIÑA COLADA FRUIT DIP

1 small package sugar-free vanilla instant
  pudding mix
8 ounces plain low-fat yogurt
1 small can juice-pack crushed pineapple
¾ cup skim milk
1 tablespoon pineapple extract
1 tablespoon banana extract
2 tablespoons coconut extract
¼ teaspoon almond extract

Combine first 4 ingredients in blender container. Process until smooth. Add flavorings. Process for 30 seconds. Pour into airtight container. Chill overnight. Add a small amount of additional milk to make of desired consistency if necessary. Serve with assorted bite-sized fruit.

Yield: 8 to 12 servings

LOW-CAL VEGETABLE SALAD

½ cup vinegar
½ cup oil
½ cup sugar
4 packets artificial sweetener
1 teaspoon salt
½ teaspoon pepper
1 can Le Sueur peas
2 cans whole kernel corn
1 can French-style green beans
1 small jar chopped pimento
1 green bell pepper
1 medium onion
½ cup chopped celery
½ head cauliflower

Combine first 6 ingredients in saucepan. Bring to a boil; remove from heat. Let stand until completely cool. Drain peas, corn, green beans and pimento in colander for several minutes. Chop fresh vegetables. Combine canned and fresh vegetables in large wide-mouth jar. Add vinegar mixture; cover tightly. Turn jar over several times to mix. Marinate in refrigerator for several hours to several days. Drain well before serving.

Yield: 12 servings

BARBECUE SLAW

4 quarts grated cabbage
3 large onions, grated
2 green bell peppers, chopped
3 carrots, grated
3 cups sugar
1 cup white vinegar
1 tablespoon salt
1 teaspoon pepper
1½ teaspoons cayenne pepper
3 cups prepared mustard

Combine all ingredients in stockpot. Bring to a boil. Boil for 20 minutes. Ladle into hot sterilized jars; seal with 2-piece lids.

Yield: 9 pints

DASHED POTATOES

8 medium potatoes
1 large onion, chopped
½ teaspoon salt
½ teaspoon pepper
1 teaspoon Mrs. Dash original salt-free
*   seasoning*
1 tablespoon margarine

Scrub potatoes; do not peel. Cut each potato into 8 pieces. Mix potatoes and onion in 2-quart casserole. Sprinkle with seasonings; mix well. Dot with margarine. Microwave, covered, on High for 15 minutes or until potatoes are tender.

Yield: 6 servings

TERIYAKI PINWHEELS

1 tablespoon olive oil
½ cup soy sauce
¼ cup sugar
2 tablespoons orange juice
1 teaspoon ginger
½ teaspoon salt
2 to 3 pounds flank steak
Pineapple slices

Combine first 6 ingredients in small bowl. Cut steak cross grain into ¾-inch strips. Roll up 2 or 3 slices to make pinwheel; secure with skewer or wooden picks. Repeat with remaining steak. Place in shallow dish. Pour soy sauce mixture over pinwheels. Marinate, covered, in refrigerator for 2 hours to overnight. Drain, reserving marinade. Grill over medium coals for 5 to 7 minutes. Turn pinwheels over; brush with reserved marinade. Grill for 2 to 3 minutes. Place pineapple slice on each. Grill for 3 to 4 minutes longer; brush with marinade.

Yield: 4 to 6 servings

LOW-CAL CHICKEN

1 chicken, quartered
1 teaspoon garlic salt
2 teaspoons paprika
½ teaspoon oregano
¼ teaspoon white pepper
1 teaspoon minced parsley
½ cup lemon juice
½ cup water
¼ cup vegetable oil (optional)

Place chicken in large shallow glass baking dish. Sprinkle with spices and parsley. Pour mixture of lemon juice, water and oil over top. Microwave on High for 15 minutes. Drain, reserving marinade. Grill over medium coals for 20 minutes or until tender, turning and basting frequently with reserved marinade.

Prepare Low-Calorie Grilled Fish by reducing paprika to 1 teaspoon and omitting water. Microwaving is not necessary but select large fillets of even thickness and grill for 20 minutes, turning and basting frequently with marinade.

Yield: 4 servings

BANANA FROZEN YOGURT

3 bananas
½ cup strawberry yogurt
5 frozen strawberries
½ teaspoon vanilla extract

Slice bananas; place in freezer container. Freeze for 24 hours. Combine frozen bananas, yogurt, frozen strawberries and vanilla in food processor. Process until smooth, scraping side of container if necessary. May store in freezer for up to 4 hours. May substitute plain yogurt for strawberry yogurt for fewer calories.

Yield: 4 servings

STEAK ROLL BROIL

1/3 cup sliced mushrooms
1 tablespoon chopped green onions
2 teaspoons margarine
1/3 cup sour cream
1 teaspoon chopped parsley
Salt to taste
6 slices beef tenderloin
2 tablespoons butter
1 teaspoon chopped parsley
Garlic powder to taste
6 hot dog buns

Sauté mushrooms and green onions in margarine in skillet until tender; remove from heat. Add sour cream, 1 teaspoon parsley and salt; mix well. Flatten each tenderloin slice to 4-inch square. Spread with mushroom mixture; roll up and secure with wooden picks. Grill 3 inches from hot coals for rare, 4 inches for medium or 5 to 6 inches for well done, turning and basting frequently with mixture of butter, 1 teaspoon parsley and garlic powder. Serve on buns.

Yield: 6 servings

BASIC MARINATED STEAK

3 dashes of Worcestershire sauce
3 tablespoons vegetable oil
3 tablespoons vinegar
1/4 teaspoon oregano
1/8 teaspoon pepper
1 clove of garlic, minced
2 pounds steak

Combine first 6 ingredients in large bowl. Let stand for 15 minutes to blend seasonings. Add steak. Pierce with fork. Turn steak to coat well with seasonings. Marinate for 4 to 5 hours. Drain, reserving marinade. Grill steak 4 inches from hot coals until done to taste, turning and basting with marinade occasionally.

Yield: 3 to 4 servings

BEEF ALAMO

1 pound beef flank steak
1/2 cup hot mustard
8 to 12 flour tortillas
2 medium tomatoes, finely chopped
1 medium red onion, finely chopped
1 (4-ounce) can green chili peppers, finely chopped

Score steak diagonally at 1-inch intervals on both sides, making diamond-shaped pattern. Spread mustard on both sides of steak. Chill, covered, for several hours. Grill steak over medium-hot coals for 8 to 10 minutes on each side. Stack tortillas; wrap in foil. Place on edge of grill to warm. Cut steak into thin slices. Spoon into warm tortillas. Top with mixture of tomatoes, onion and chili peppers. Roll up tortillas.

Yield: 4 to 6 servings

GRILLED RIB-EYE STEAKS

4 rib-eye steaks
Lemon pepper seasoning to taste
Salt to taste
8 teaspoons Italian salad dressing

Sprinkle steaks with lemon pepper and salt on both sides. Spread 1 teaspoon Italian dressing on each side of steaks. Place steaks in dish. Marinate in refrigerator for 1 to 2 hours. Preheat coals for 20 to 30 minutes or until hot. Place steaks on grill. Cook until done to taste, turning occasionally.

Yield: 4 servings

OUTDOOR LORE

Roast large green bell peppers over hot coals until charred on all sides, turning frequently. Peel, discard seed and membrane and slice into strips.

GRILLED STEAK

3 pounds 2-inch thick round steak
Meat tenderizer
1 cup water
¼ cup soy sauce
¼ cup packed brown sugar
¼ cup lemon juice
1 tablespoon Worcestershire sauce
1 tablespoon minced parsley
¼ teaspoon hot sauce

Sprinkle steak generously with meat tenderizer. Combine remaining ingredients in shallow bowl; mix well. Add steak. Marinate, covered, in refrigerator overnight. Drain, reserving marinade. Place steak on grill rack 6 inches from hot coals. Grill for 15 minutes, basting occasionally with reserved marinade. Turn. Grill for 15 minutes, basting occasionally. Grill for 10 minutes on each side for rare steak or 25 minutes on each side for well done steak.

Yield: 6 servings

MEAL IN A PACKET

2 pounds round steak, cut into 1-inch pieces
2 onions, chopped
5 carrots, chopped
2 potatoes, chopped
1 (4-ounce) can mushroom pieces
1 can cream of mushroom soup
½ soup can water
Salt and pepper to taste

Combine steak, onions, carrots, potatoes, mushrooms, soup, water, salt and pepper in bowl; mix well. Let stand for 10 minutes. Spoon onto five 18-inch foil squares; seal foil to make 5-inch packets. Cook with lid down over low heat for 15 minutes on each side.

Yield: 5 servings

MARINATED CHUCK ROAST

1 (4- to 6-pound) chuck roast
Meat tenderizer
Garlic powder to taste
2 tablespoons corn oil
¼ cup catsup
½ cup orange juice
½ cup red wine vinegar
2 tablespoons Worcestershire sauce
2 tablespoons soy sauce
½ teaspoon pepper

Sprinkle roast generously with meat tenderizer and garlic powder. Marinate roast in mixture of remaining ingredients in covered shallow dish in refrigerator for 24 hours, turning occasionally. Sprinkle with additional tenderizer. Let stand at room temperature for 30 minutes. Grill over medium coals until done to taste.

Yield: 6 to 8 servings

GINGERY FLANK STEAK

½ cup soy sauce
¼ cup sugar
2 tablespoons vinegar
1 clove of garlic, minced
1 teaspoon ginger
1 (1-pound) flank steak

Combine first 5 ingredients in shallow dish; mix well. Add steak. Marinate, covered, in refrigerator for 8 hours. Drain, reserving marinade. Grill over medium coals for 8 to 10 minutes on each side, basting with reserved marinade occasionally. Slice cross grain.

Yield: 4 servings

OUTDOOR LORE

Children love to eat any food on a stick, such as fruit, vegetables or hot dogs.

GRILLED TENDERLOIN

1 (2-pound) beef tenderloin
1 (12-ounce) bottle of Italian salad dressing

Combine tenderloin with dressing in large plastic bag; seal well. Refrigerate overnight, turning several times. Remove from refrigerator 2 hours before cooking; drain well. Grill over hot coals for 40 minutes for medium-rare or 50 minutes for medium.

Yield: 8 servings

BARBECUED BEEF BRISKET

1 (6-pound) beef brisket
¾ cup red wine vinegar
½ cup packed brown sugar
½ cup unsweetened pineapple juice
⅓ cup molasses
⅓ cup prepared mustard
1 tablespoon minced onion
3 tablespoons Worcestershire sauce
1 teaspoon chili powder
¼ teaspoon hot sauce

Place brisket in zip-lock heavy-duty bag. Combine remaining ingredients in bowl. Pour over brisket; seal bag securely. Shake bag gently to coat brisket. Place bag in shallow container. Marinate in refrigerator for 4 hours or longer, turning bag occasionally. Drain, reserving marinade. Place brisket on grill over medium-hot coals. Grill until brown, turning once. Close lid. Grill for 15 minutes. Turn brisket; baste with reserved marinade. Place brisket in center of large piece of heavy-duty foil. Bring foil up to enclose brisket, gathering loosely at top to leave opening. Pour remaining reserved marinade into opening. Press opening in foil to seal tightly. Place on grill; close lid. Grill over medium coals for 1½ to 2 hours or until very tender. Cut cross grain into thin slices.

Yield: 12 servings

TERIYAKI STEAK

½ cup water
½ cup soy sauce
1 tablespoon brown sugar
1½ teaspoons ginger
2 pounds 1½-inch thick sirloin steak

Combine first 4 ingredients in saucepan. Bring to a boil. Let stand until cool. Score steak on both sides; place in shallow dish. Pour soy sauce mixture over steak. Chill, covered with plastic wrap, for 2 hours or longer, turning occasionally. Grill 2 to 3 inches above hot coals for 7 minutes on each side.

Yield: 8 servings

GRILLED LONDON BROIL

1 teaspoon salt
½ teaspoon pepper
¼ teaspoon basil
¼ teaspoon rosemary
2 cloves of garlic, pressed
½ medium onion, chopped
2 tablespoons red wine vinegar
¼ cup vegetable oil
1 (1- to 1½-pound) flank steak

Combine salt, pepper, basil, rosemary, garlic, onion, red wine vinegar and oil in bowl; mix well. Place steak in shallow glass dish. Pour vinegar mixture over steak. Marinate, covered with plastic wrap, in refrigerator for 2 hours or longer, turning once. Remove steak, reserving marinade. Grill steak over hot coals for 15 minutes or to desired degree of doneness, turning once. Carve diagonally cross grain into thin slices. Heat reserved marinade; drizzle over steak.

Yield: 4 to 6 servings

MARINATED ROAST SIRLOIN

1 (5-pound) sirloin roast
1 tablespoon meat tenderizer
½ cup strong coffee
½ cup soy sauce
1 tablespoon Worcestershire sauce
1 tablespoon vinegar
1 onion, thinly sliced

Place roast in shallow dish. Sprinkle with tenderizer; pierce with fork. Combine coffee, soy sauce, Worcestershire sauce and vinegar in bowl; mix well. Pour over roast. Arrange onion over top. Let stand at room temperature for several hours. Roast must be at room temperature before grilling. Grill, with lid closed, over hot coals for 45 to 60 minutes or to desired degree of doneness, turning once.

Yield: 8 servings

GRILLED SIRLOIN TIP

1 (3- to 4-pound) sirloin tip
Meat tenderizer
Garlic powder, pepper and Mrs. Dash
    seasoning to taste

Preheat coals for 30 minutes. Push charcoal to side of grill. Sprinkle sirloin with tenderizer using package directions. Season to taste. Place to 1 side of charcoal. Close lid. Cook for 15 minutes. Rotate sirloin so the same side is down but outer edge is now next to charcoal. Cook for 15 minutes. Turn roast; place over charcoal. Insert meat thermometer. Cook until done to taste. Cut into thin slices.

Yield: 8 servings

MARINATED ROUND STEAK

½ cup soy sauce
⅓ cup vegetable oil
1 teaspoon ginger
1 teaspoon dry mustard
½ teaspoon garlic powder
1 (2-pound) round steak

Combine soy sauce, oil, ginger, dry mustard and garlic powder in bowl; mix well. Pour over steak in shallow dish. Chill, covered, for 2 to 4 hours. Grill steak over hot coals until done to taste. Slice steak cross grain to serve.

Yield: 8 servings

ENGLISH BEEF RIB BARBECUE

1 pounds English beef ribs or baby beef back
    ribs
¼ cup teriyaki sauce
3 tablespoons Worcestershire sauce
3 tablespoons rice vinegar
¼ cup sugar
½ teaspoon salt
¼ teaspoon pepper
½ teaspoon five-spices powder
1 tablespoon sesame seed
1 teaspoon minced garlic

Score ribs between bones. Place ribs in shallow dish. Combine remaining ingredients in bowl; stir until sugar dissolves. Pour marinade over ribs. Marinate, covered, in refrigerator overnight, turning and basting occasionally. Place bone side down over high heat. Grill until crispy and brown or done to taste, turning once.

Yield: 3 to 4 servings

BARBECUED BEEF SHORT RIBS

3 pounds beef short ribs
1/2 cup vinegar
1 envelope dry onion soup mix
1/4 cup sugar
2 tablespoons prepared brown mustard
1 1/2 cups catsup
1/2 cup vegetable oil
1/2 cup vinegar
Hot pepper sauce to taste

Place ribs in Dutch oven. Add 1/2 cup vinegar and enough water to cover. Bring to a boil. Simmer, covered, for 45 minutes. Combine soup mix, sugar and mustard in bowl; mix well. Stir in catsup, oil, 1/2 cup vinegar and hot pepper sauce. Bring mixture to a boil. Simmer for 20 minutes. Place ribs on grill over hot coals. Brown on all sides. Cook for 25 minutes, basting with sauce occasionally.

Yield: 6 servings

BEEF KABOBS

1 cup vegetable oil
1 cup wine vinegar
2 teaspoons onion powder
2 teaspoons garlic powder
1 teaspoon oregano
1 tablespoon dried mint
Salt and pepper to taste
3 pounds lean beef, cut up
2 (16-ounce) cans small whole potatoes
1 pound mushrooms
2 green bell peppers, cut up
3 onions, cut into wedges

Combine first 8 ingredients in sealable plastic bag; mix well. Add beef. Marinate for 3 hours or longer. Drain. Alternate beef, potatoes, mushrooms, green peppers and onions on skewers. Cook over hot coals until beef is cooked through, turning frequently. Serve with pita bread.

Yield: 8 servings

KOREAN SIRLOIN SKEWERS

1 pound 2-inch thick sirloin
1/4 cup soy sauce
1/4 cup sugar
2 green onions, finely chopped
2 cloves of garlic, crushed
1/2 teaspoon instant chicken bouillon
1/2 teaspoon pepper
2 tablespoons vegetable oil

Cut beef cross grain into 1/8- to 1/4-inch thick slices. Mix next 6 ingredients in bowl. Add beef and oil; mix well. Marinate, covered, in refrigerator for 1 hour or longer; drain. Thread beef loosely onto skewers. Place on grill over hot coals. Grill until brown on both sides.

Yield: 4 servings

MARINATED KABOBS

1/2 cup vegetable oil
1 tablespoon cider vinegar
2 tablespoons fresh lemon juice
2 tablespoons finely chopped onion
1 small clove of garlic, minced
1 teaspoon chili powder
1/2 teaspoon each poultry seasoning, oregano
    and ginger
2 teaspoons salt
1/4 teaspoon pepper
2 pounds sirloin steak cubes
12 each cherry tomatoes and small onions
2 green bell peppers, cut into 1-inch pieces

Mix oil, vinegar, lemon juice, onion, garlic, chili powder, poultry seasoning, oregano, ginger, salt and pepper in bowl. Add steak cubes; mix well. Marinate, covered, in refrigerator overnight or at room temperature for 3 to 4 hours. Thread steak cubes onto skewers alternately with cherry tomatoes, small onions and green pepper pieces. Grill for 15 minutes or until done to taste, turning frequently. Serve with rice or baked potatoes.

Yield: 6 servings

Famous Shish Kabobs

½ cup catsup
1 teaspoon salt
2 tablespoons sugar
2 tablespoons each steak sauce and vinegar
¼ cup water
2 tablespoons shortening
2 tablespoons Worcestershire sauce
1½ pounds steak, cut into cubes
8 large onion wedges
8 large pieces of green bell pepper
8 each cherry tomatoes and mushrooms
8 pineapple chunks

Combine first 8 ingredients in saucepan. Bring to a boil. Place steak cubes in heatproof bowl. Pour sauce over steak. Marinate, covered, in refrigerator for several hours to overnight. Drain, reserving marinade. Thread steak onto skewers alternately with vegetables and pineapple. Grill over hot coals to desired degree of doneness, basting with reserved marinade.

Yield: 4 servings

Fiesta Beef Kabobs

¼ cup dry onion soup mix
2 tablespoons sugar
½ cup catsup
¼ cup corn oil
1 tablespoon prepared mustard
½ cup water
¼ cup vinegar
¼ teaspoon salt
1 beef sirloin tip, cut into 1-inch cubes
1 green bell pepper, chopped
1 red bell pepper, chopped
Mushrooms
Cherry tomatoes
Small onions, slightly cooked

Combine soup mix, sugar, catsup, corn oil, prepared mustard, water, vinegar and salt in saucepan; mix well. Bring to a boil; reduce heat.

Simmer for 20 minutes. Let cool. Add beef and toss to coat. Marinate, covered, in the refrigerator overnight. Let stand at room temperature for 1 hour. Drain, reserving marinade. Thread beef, green pepper, red pepper, mushrooms and onions alternately onto 4 skewers. Broil over medium coals to desired degree of doneness, brushing frequently with reserved marinade.

Yield: 4 servings

Mexican Kabobs

1 tablespoon vinegar
1 tablespoon water
1 envelope Italian salad dressing mix
1 teaspoon chili powder
1 tablespoon vegetable oil
⅓ cup orange juice
1 pound round steak
1 large green bell pepper
1 large onion
12 large cherry tomatoes

Combine vinegar, water, salad dressing mix and chili powder in jar with tight-fitting lid; shake well. Add oil and orange juice; shake well. Cut steak into cubes. Combine with marinade in glass dish. Marinate, covered, in refrigerator overnight. Drain, reserving marinade. Cut green pepper into chunks. Cut onion into 12 wedges. Thread steak, green pepper, onion and cherry tomatoes alternately onto 4 skewers. Grill over hot coals for 4 to 5 minutes on each side, brushing frequently with marinade.

Yield: 4 servings

Outdoor Lore

Clean grill with crumpled foil before lighting coals for grilling.

SIRLOIN KABOBS

3 pounds round or sirloin steak
Whole fresh mushrooms
Juice of 1½ lemons
3 tablespoons vegetable oil
1 medium onion, grated
1 teaspoon salt
¼ teaspoon ginger
2 teaspoons Worcestershire sauce
1 bay leaf, crushed
1 clove of garlic, crushed
½ teaspoon dry mustard
2 green bell peppers, cut up
2 large onions, cut into wedges
2 cans whole white potatoes

Cut steak into cubes. Remove stems from mushrooms. Place steak and mushrooms in bowl. Combine lemon juice, oil, grated onion, salt, ginger, Worcestershire sauce, bay leaf, garlic and dry mustard in bowl; mix well. Pour over steak. Marinate, covered, in refrigerator for 4 hours to overnight. Drain, reserving marinade. Thread steak, mushrooms, green peppers, onions and potatoes alternately onto skewers. Grill over hot coals for 15 to 20 minutes or to desired degree of doneness, turning and basting frequently with reserved marinade.

Yield: 8 servings

STEAK STRIPS EN BROCHETTE

2 pounds round steak
1 cup Russian salad dressing
2 tablespoons lemon juice
15 medium fresh mushrooms
15 cherry tomatoes

Cut steak into ¼-inch thick strips; place in plastic bag. Combine salad dressing and lemon juice in bowl; mix well. Pour into bag with steak. Press out air; seal bag securely. Marinate in refrigerator for 4 hours to overnight. Drain, reserving marinade.

Thread beef strips alternately with mushrooms and tomatoes onto 15-inch skewers. Place skewers on grill. Cook over medium coals for 3 minutes, brushing with marinade occasionally. Turn. Cook for 3 to 4 minutes or until done to taste, brushing with marinade occasionally.

Yield: 4 to 6 servings

TERIYAKI KABOBS

½ cup soy sauce
½ cup packed brown sugar
1 clove of garlic, crushed
1 tablespoon grated ginger
1 tablespoon vegetable oil
1 tablespoon orange juice
1 (3-pound) sirloin steak, cut into cubes

Combine soy sauce, brown sugar, garlic, ginger, oil and orange juice in small bowl; mix well. Place beef in shallow dish. Pour marinade over beef. Marinate in refrigerator for 8 hours to overnight, turning occasionally. Thread beef onto skewers. Grill until done to taste. Marinade is also good on chicken and pork.

Yield: 6 servings

FOIL PACKET HOBO DINNER

1 pound ground chuck
2 potatoes, sliced
1 large onion, sliced
Salt and pepper to taste

Shape ground chuck into 2 large patties. Place each on large piece of heavy-duty foil. Layer potatoes and onion on patties. Season with salt and pepper. Seal foil securely. Place each packet on grill. Cook over hot coals for 1 hour or to desired degree of doneness.

Yield: 2 servings

Hobo Burgers

1 1/2 pounds ground beef
Salt and pepper to taste
1/2 cup shredded Cheddar cheese
1/2 cup shredded Swiss cheese
1 (4-ounce) can sliced mushrooms, drained
4 slices bacon
4 hamburger buns

Preheat coals. Combine ground beef, salt and pepper in bowl; mix well. Shape into 8 patties between waxed paper. Place cheese and mushrooms in center of 4 patties. Top with remaining patties. Press around edges to seal. Wrap each patty with bacon; secure with wooden pick. Grill over hot coals for 14 minutes or to desired degree of doneness. Serve on hamburger buns.

Yield: 4 servings

Oriental Burgers

1/2 cup soy sauce
2 tablespoons sugar
1 teaspoon crushed gingerroot
1 clove of garlic, crushed
1 pound ground beef
3 tablespoons butter, softened
4 hamburger buns, split

Combine soy sauce, sugar, gingerroot and garlic in small bowl; mix well. Shape ground beef into 4 patties. Place in shallow glass dish. Pour soy sauce mixture over patties. Marinate, covered, in refrigerator for 30 minutes. Drain, reserving marinade. Place patties on grill. Grill 4 inches from hot coals for 7 minutes on each side, basting with reserved marinade several times. Serve in buttered hamburger buns. May substitute 1/4 teaspoon ground ginger for gingerroot.

Yield: 4 servings

Everyday Drumsticks

1 pound ground beef
1 egg, beaten
1 teaspoon salt
12 saltine crackers, crushed
3 slices bacon, sliced lengthwise and crosswise

Combine ground beef, egg and salt in bowl; mix well. Divide into 6 portions. Shape around wooden skewers. Roll "drumsticks" in cracker crumbs. Place on foil. Cover with bacon. Place on grill. Cook over hot coals for 30 minutes or until done to taste.

Yield: 6 servings

Party-Perfect Pizza

1 (10-ounce) can pizza sauce
8 ounces ground beef, cooked
1 cup shredded mozzarella cheese
1 teaspoon onion powder
1 teaspoon oregano
1/2 teaspoon salt
1/4 to 1/2 teaspoon garlic powder
6 English muffins, split
Parmesan cheese to taste

Reserve 1/2 cup pizza sauce. Mix remaining pizza sauce, ground beef, mozzarella cheese, onion powder, oregano, salt and garlic powder in bowl. Place English muffin halves cut side down on baking sheet. Spread reserved pizza sauce evenly over muffin halves. Spoon ground beef mixture on each muffin, spreading to edges. Sprinkle with Parmesan cheese. Place on warming rack of preheated gas grill. Cook with lid down over low to medium heat for 10 to 20 minutes or until brown and bubbly.

Yield: 12 servings

Barbecued Lamb

1 (6-pound) leg of lamb
1½ cups apple juice
1 teaspoon (heaping) poultry seasoning
1 teaspoon garlic liquid
1 teaspoon garlic salt
¼ teaspoon pepper

Have butcher butterfly lamb and remove bone. Open lamb; place in large roaster. Mix remaining ingredients in saucepan. Bring to a boil. Pour over lamb, turning lamb to coat both sides. Marinate, covered, in refrigerator for 8 hours to overnight, turning occasionally. Place fat side down on grill. Barbecue over hot coals for 45 minutes to 1 hour, turning and basting every 15 minutes.

Yield: 16 servings

Marinated Skewered Lamb

3 pounds lamb, cut into 2-inch cubes
2 onions, cut into quarters
3 green bell peppers, cut into quarters
8 ounces cherry tomatoes, cut into halves
1 cup apple juice
½ cup olive oil
¼ cup lemon juice
2 cloves of garlic, crushed
3 tablespoons oregano
Salt and pepper to taste

Divide lamb into 8 portions. Thread each portion onto skewer alternately with onions, bell peppers and cherry tomatoes. Combine remaining ingredients in bowl; mix well. Place skewers in dish. Cover with marinade. Refrigerate, covered, overnight. Grill over hot coals for 20 minutes, turning frequently. Serve over rice.

Yield: 4 to 6 servings

Barbecued Butterflied Lamb

2 pounds leg of lamb, boned, butterflied
½ to 1 cup lemon juice
¾ to 1 cup olive oil
¼ cup chopped garlic
Salt and pepper to taste

Remove all fat and tendon running through lamb. Cut into serving pieces. Place in dish. Combine remaining ingredients in bowl; mix well. Pour over lamb; pierce lamb with two-tined fork. Marinate, covered, in refrigerator for 12 hours, turning occasionally. Drain, reserving marinade. Place lamb in hinged grill. Cook for 10 to 20 minutes or until done to taste.

Yield: 4 servings

Barbecued Rack of Lamb

1 (1½-pound) rack of lamb
2 teaspoons salt
1 teaspoon each lemon pepper seasoning,
   garlic salt and rosemary

Rub lamb on all sides with mixture of seasonings. Chill for 6 hours. Preheat grill to 350 degrees. Cook, covered, over indirect heat for 1 hour.

Yield: 4 servings

Ground Lamb Kabobs

1½ pounds ground lamb, beef or veal
¼ cup each chopped parsley and mint leaves
1 large onion, minced
2 cloves of garlic, minced
Dash of red pepper flakes
1 egg

Combine all ingredients in bowl; mix well. Shape by ¼ cupfuls into 4-inch rolls. Thread 2 or 3 rolls lengthwise through center onto each of six 15-inch skewers. Grill over medium-hot coals to desired degree of doneness, turning frequently.

Yield: 6 servings

GRILLED MARINATED PORK

1 clove of garlic, minced
4 green onions and tops, chopped
¼ cup margarine
2 tablespoons lemon juice
1 teaspoon lemon rind
½ cup packed brown sugar
¼ cup vinegar
¼ cup water
½ cup catsup
1 tablespoon Worcestershire sauce
2 dashes of hot pepper sauce
2 pounds boneless pork roast, cut into ¾-inch
   slices

Sauté garlic and green onions in margarine in skillet for 5 minutes. Add lemon juice, lemon rind, brown sugar, vinegar, water, catsup, Worcestershire sauce and hot pepper sauce; mix well. Bring just to a boil. Pour over pork roast in casserole. Marinate, covered, in refrigerator for 3 hours or longer. Drain, reserving marinade. Grill over medium-hot coals for 30 minutes, basting with marinade frequently.

Yield: 4 servings

BEST-EVER PORK CHOPS

4 pork chops
1 bottle of Worcestershire sauce
Cavender's Greek Seasoning to taste

Place pork chops in shallow dish. Pour Worcestershire sauce over top. Marinate, covered, in refrigerator for 1 hour. Sprinkle Greek Seasoning on both sides of pork chops. Grill over hot coals for 30 minutes or until tender.

Yield: 4 servings

TERIYAKI PORK CHOPS

½ cup teriyaki sauce
¼ cup minced green onions
¼ cup lemon juice
2 tablespoons peanut oil
4 cloves of garlic, minced
2 teaspoons crushed red pepper
4 (¾-inch) pork chops

Combine teriyaki sauce, green onions, lemon juice, peanut oil, garlic and red pepper in small bowl; mix well. Place pork chops in shallow dish. Pour marinade over pork chops. Chill for 4 hours to overnight, turning pork chops occasionally. Drain, reserving marinade. Place 6 to 8 inches above hot coals. Grill for 30 to 45 minutes or until cooked through, turning and basting frequently with reserved marinade.

Yield: 4 servings

MARINATED PORK CHOPS

1 (6-ounce) can frozen lemonade concentrate,
   thawed
⅔ cup soy sauce
½ teaspoon garlic salt
¼ teaspoon celery salt
¼ teaspoon onion salt
4 medium pork chops

Combine lemonade concentrate, soy sauce, garlic salt, celery salt and onion salt in bowl; mix well. Pour over pork chops in shallow dish. Marinate, covered, in refrigerator overnight. Place pork chops on grill over hot coals. Cook for 10 to 15 minutes on each side or until tender.

Yield: 4 servings

FABULOUS RIBS

Country-style pork ribs
Barbecue sauce

Rinse ribs. Brown on both sides on grill over hot coals. Place in baking pan. Cover completely with barbecue sauce. Cover with foil. Cook on grill over low coals for 5 to 6 hours.

Yield: variable

GRILLED COUNTRY-STYLE RIBS

2 to 3 pounds country-style ribs
Salt, pepper and seasoned salt to taste

Season ribs with salt, pepper and seasoned salt. Place on grill. Cook over hot coals for 45 minutes, turning frequently. Serve with or without barbecue sauce.

Yield: 4 servings

LONE STAR RIBS

3 pounds small pork ribs
1 teaspoon pepper
1 teaspoon paprika
1 tablespoon salt
2 cups catsup
3 cups water
⅓ cup flour
1 tablespoon salt
4 teaspoons sugar
2½ teaspoons paprika
1½ teaspoons pepper
1½ teaspoons chili powder
1 tablespoon prepared mustard
1½ teaspoons liquid smoke
1 cup Worcestershire sauce

Season ribs lightly on both sides with mixture of 1 teaspoon pepper, 1 teaspoon paprika and 1 tablespoon salt. Place ribs on grill or any type covered smoker or barbecue pit. Keep away from direct heat so that smoke does cooking. Cook very slowly for 1½ to 2 hours or until meat comes away from bone easily. Combine catsup and water in large saucepan; mix well. Bring to a boil. Mix dry ingredients in bowl. Add prepared mustard, liquid smoke and ½ cup Worcestershire sauce to dry mixture; mix well. Add remaining Worcestershire sauce. Add to heated mixture. Simmer for 20 minutes. Brush over ribs. Cook for 15 minutes. Store remaining sauce in refrigerator.

Yield: 4 servings

SMOKED VENISON

1 (6-ounce) can pineapple juice
2 tablespoons soy sauce or Worcestershire
* sauce*
2 tablespoons sugar
2 teaspoons sesame oil
2 teaspoons MSG
1 teaspoon garlic powder
½ teaspoon pepper
2 green onions, chopped
1 (4- to 5-pound) venison roast
3 to 5 cloves of garlic
1 to 2 tablespoons Cavender's Seasoning
6 or 8 slices bacon

Combine pineapple juice, soy sauce, sugar, oil, MSG, garlic powder, pepper and green onions in bowl. Add venison. Marinate, covered, in refrigerator for 24 hours. Pierce roast in several places with sharp knife. Insert garlic cloves into roast. Rub Cavender's Seasoning on roast; wrap with bacon. Place roast on rack in smoker. Smoke for 3 to 4 hours or to 140 degrees on meat thermometer for rare, 160 degrees for medium or 170 degrees for well done.

Yield: 10 to 12 servings

EASY BARBECUED CHICKEN

1 (3-pound) chicken, cut up
Lemon pepper seasoning and salt to taste
1 teaspoon hot sauce
1 tablespoon Worcestershire sauce
1 cup barbecue sauce

Preheat coals for 20 to 30 minutes or until hot. Sprinkle chicken pieces with lemon pepper and salt. Place chicken on grill. Cook, covered, for 45 to 50 minutes or until tender, turning as needed. Mix hot sauce, Worcestershire sauce and barbecue sauce in bowl. Baste 1 side of chicken with sauce. Cook for 1 to 2 minutes longer.

Yield: 6 servings

CAFE-STYLE BARBECUE CHICKEN

3 (2½-pound) chickens
2 tablespoons vinegar
3½ cups tomato sauce
1 cup catsup
1 bay leaf
Juice of 1 lemon
¼ cup finely chopped onion
1½ teaspoons red pepper
1 teaspoon salt
1 teaspoon black pepper
¼ cup red wine vinegar
1 teaspoon pickling spice
½ teaspoon oregano
½ teaspoon garlic powder
1 teaspoon celery seed
¼ cup packed brown sugar

Cut chickens into quarters. Arrange in baking dishes. Bake at 350 degrees for 45 minutes or until brown. Drain and cool to room temperature. Combine remaining ingredients in saucepan. Bring to a boil; reduce heat. Simmer for 20 minutes, stirring frequently. Remove bay leaf. Place chicken skin side up on grill over hot coals. Grill for several minutes. Baste generously with sauce.

Turn chicken; baste generously with sauce. Grill for 10 minutes or until chicken is slightly charred.

Yield: 12 servings

GREEK CHICKEN

6 to 8 large chicken breast filets
1 cup vinegar
1 cup vegetable oil
½ teaspoon salt
½ teaspoon pepper
2 tablespoons oregano

Marinate chicken in mixture of vinegar, oil, salt, pepper and oregano in bowl in refrigerator for several hours. Grill over hot coals until golden brown.

Yield: 6 to 8 servings

MAKE-AHEAD CHICKEN

1½ cups water
1 cup catsup
1 cup sugar
½ cup vinegar
¼ cup margarine
1½ teaspoons Tabasco sauce
2 tablespoons prepared mustard
2 tablespoons salt
1 teaspoon pepper
1 chicken, cut up

Combine water, catsup, sugar, vinegar, margarine, Tabasco sauce, mustard, salt and pepper in saucepan; mix well. Bring to a boil. Add chicken pieces; reduce heat. Cook, uncovered, over low heat for 45 minutes. Chill chicken in sauce until ready to use. Grill chicken over hot coals for 5 minutes on each side or until brown.

Yield: 4 servings

BARBECUED CHICKEN

Salt and pepper to taste
4 chickens, cut into halves
2 cups margarine
1 cup lemon juice
2 tablespoons Worcestershire sauce
2 teaspoons salt
½ teaspoon pepper
6 drops of Tabasco sauce
½ cup orange juice

Sprinkle salt and pepper over chicken. Combine remaining ingredients in saucepan; mix well. Heat over low heat until margarine is melted. Brush chicken with sauce. Place chicken on grill. Cook over low coals with 2 or 3 presoaked hickory chips added for 1½ hours or until chicken is tender, turning and basting frequently.

Yield: 8 servings

CHICKEN BARBECUE

6 (8-ounce) boneless skinless chicken breasts
2 tablespoons soy sauce
1 tablespoon vegetable oil
1 tablespoon orange juice
1 clove of garlic, minced
¼ teaspoon ground ginger
¼ teaspoon Chinese five-spice seasoning

Pierce chicken with two-tined fork. Combine soy sauce, oil, orange juice, garlic, ginger and five-spice seasoning in bowl; mix well. Pour over chicken in shallow dish. Marinate, covered, in refrigerator for 12 hours or longer, turning occasionally. Drain. Place chicken in hinged grill. Cook over hot coals for 2 minutes on each side or until cooked through.

Yield: 6 servings

CHICKEN BREAST MARINADE

1 (10-ounce) bottle of teriyaki sauce
1½ cups orange juice
¾ cup peanut oil
1 teaspoon MSG
1 teaspoon garlic powder
3 to 4 pounds chicken breast filets

Combine teriyaki sauce, orange juice, peanut oil, MSG and garlic powder in bowl; mix well. Pour over chicken in shallow dish. Marinate, covered, in refrigerator overnight, turning occasionally. Grill over hot coals for 20 to 30 minutes or until golden brown, turning frequently.

Yield: 6 to 8 servings

GRILLED CHICKEN MARINADE

1 cup orange juice
⅓ cup lemon juice
¼ cup vegetable oil
1 to 2 tablespoons soy sauce
1 teaspoon lemon pepper seasoning or Italian
  seasoning
6 boneless chicken breasts

Combine orange juice, lemon juice, oil, soy sauce and lemon pepper in bowl; mix well. Add chicken to marinade, turning to coat well. Marinate, covered, in refrigerator for 2 hours to overnight. Grill chicken over hot coals for 20 minutes or until tender.

Yield: 6 servings

OUTDOOR LORE

Add orange juice and grated rind to bottled barbecue sauce for delicious homemade flavor.

Marinated Grilled Chicken

4 small chickens, split
½ cup cranberry juice cocktail
½ cup apple juice
¼ cup vegetable oil
1 tablespoon rosemary
1 teaspoon black peppercorns
½ teaspoon salt

Remove wing tips from chicken. Marinate, covered, in mixture of remaining ingredients in bowl in refrigerator for 1 hour, turning once. Drain, reserving marinade. Place skin side up on grill 5 inches from coals. Grill for 15 minutes, brushing with reserved marinade. Turn chicken. Grill until tender.

Yield: 8 servings

Chicken Yogurt Kabobs

2 pounds boneless chicken breasts
Salt and pepper to taste
½ cup yogurt
2 cloves of garlic, minced
1 shallot, minced
Grated rind of ½ lemon
2 tablespoons chopped parsley
2 tablespoons chopped mint
1 tablespoon lemon juice

Rub chicken with salt and pepper. Combine yogurt, garlic, shallot, lemon rind, parsley, mint and lemon juice in large bowl; mix well. Add chicken. Marinate, covered, in refrigerator for 2 hours. Drain, reserving marinade. Thread chicken accordion-style onto skewers, shaking off excess marinade. Place on grill over medium coals. Cook until no longer pink, turning and basting occasionally with reserved marinade.

Yield: 6 servings

Chicken Kabobs

6 chicken breast filets
24 squares of green bell pepper
2 tomatoes, cut into wedges
1 (12-ounce) package mushroom caps
1 cup soy sauce
½ cup corn vegetable oil
¼ cup sugar
4 teaspoons lemon juice
1 teaspoon meat tenderizer
2 cloves of garlic

Preheat grill. Cut chicken into 2-inch pieces. Thread chicken and vegetables onto skewers. Combine soy sauce and remaining ingredients in bowl; mix well. Place skewers on foil over hot coals. Grill for 30 minutes, basting frequently with sauce.

Yield: 6 servings

Chicken Liver Kabobs

1 pound chicken livers
¼ cup freshly chopped parsley
½ teaspoon red pepper flakes
1 small onion, thinly sliced
1 clove of garlic, minced
Salt and black pepper to taste

Place chicken in bowl. Add parsley, red pepper flakes, onion, garlic, salt and black pepper; toss gently. Marinate, covered, in refrigerator for 2 hours to overnight. Drain, reserving marinade. Thread onto skewers; place in shallow dish. Chill, covered, until ready to cook. Grill over medium-hot coals for 10 minutes or until livers are cooked through, turning and basting frequently with reserved marinade.

Yield: 4 to 6 servings

LEMON-GARLIC CHICKEN

¼ cup margarine
2 tablespoons lemon juice
⅛ teaspoon garlic powder
⅛ teaspoon pepper
4 chicken breasts

Melt margarine in saucepan. Add next 3 ingredients; mix well. Baste chicken on all sides with margarine mixture. Place chicken on grill over hot coals. Cook for about 10 minutes or until the bottom side is lightly browned; turn. Baste top side with basting mixture. Repeat process until chicken is tender. To shorten cooking time, preheat chicken in microwave until slightly warm.

Yield: 4 servings

LEMON-PEPPER CHICKEN

1 (3-pound) chicken, cut up
2 teaspoons garlic salt
2 teaspoons lemon pepper seasoning
¼ cup lemon juice
Paprika to taste

Rinse chicken pieces; pat dry. Sprinkle chicken with garlic salt and lemon pepper on both sides. Place in bowl. Pour lemon juice over chicken. Chill, covered, for several hours. Drain, reserving marinade. Preheat gas grill. Place chicken skin side up on grill. Cook, covered, over low to medium heat for 50 to 55 minutes or until tender, turning and basting every 10 minutes. Sprinkle with paprika.

Yield: 6 servings

MEXICAN CHICKEN

6 chicken breasts, skinned, boned
⅓ cup olive oil
Juice of 3 limes
4 cloves of garlic, minced
3 tablespoons chopped fresh cilantro
½ teaspoon pepper

Place chicken in shallow dish. Combine olive oil, lime juice, garlic, cilantro and pepper in bowl; mix well. Pour over chicken. Marinate, covered, in refrigerator for 1 hour; drain. Grill over hot coals on each side for 8 minutes or until tender.

Yield: 6 servings

MINTED CHICKEN

¼ cup fresh lemon juice
2 teaspoons chopped fresh mint
3 cloves of garlic, crushed
1 cup plain yogurt
1 teaspoon salt
¼ teaspoon (or less) red pepper
4 chicken breasts

Combine lemon juice, mint, garlic, yogurt, salt and red pepper in bowl; mix well. Add chicken. Marinate, covered, in refrigerator for 1 hour to overnight. Drain marinade. Grill over coals for 20 minutes or until tender.

Yield: 4 servings

TERIYAKI CHICKEN

¾ cup chopped onion
2 cloves of garlic, minced
Pinch of ground ginger
2½ tablespoons sugar
½ cup soy sauce
1 cup water
1 chicken, cut up

Combine onion, garlic, ginger, sugar, soy sauce and water in bowl; mix well. Place chicken in shallow dish. Pour sauce over chicken. Marinate in refrigerator for 12 to 14 hours. Remove chicken, discarding marinade. Cook on grill over hot coals for 45 minutes or until tender.

Yield: 4 servings

PEANUT CHICKEN SKEWERS

½ cup creamy peanut butter
½ cup peanut oil
½ cup soy sauce
½ cup packed light brown sugar
¼ cup lemon juice
2 cloves of garlic, crushed
1 tablespoon ground coriander
Cayenne pepper and salt to taste
12 chicken thigh filets, skinned

Combine peanut butter, peanut oil, soy sauce, brown sugar, lemon juice, garlic, coriander, cayenne pepper and salt in bowl; mix well. Slice chicken into 1-inch wide strips. Add to peanut butter mixture. Marinate, covered, in refrigerator for 1 hour or longer. Thread onto 12-inch bamboo skewers. Grill over hot coals until brown, basting with marinade. Serve with rice. May marinate whole chicken thighs and bake in 9×13-inch baking dish at 350 degrees for 50 to 60 minutes.

Yield: 4 servings

GRILLED CORNISH HENS

6 Cornish game hens
1 teaspoon salt
½ teaspoon pepper
3 tablespoons lemon juice
1 teaspoon rosemary
½ cup melted butter

Truss hens. Rub with salt and pepper. Arrange lengthwise on rotisserie spit. Combine lemon juice, rosemary and butter in bowl; mix well. Grill hens over hot coals for 1¼ hours, basting with sauce every 15 minutes.

Yield: 6 servings

FRIED WILD TURKEY

1 whole onion
1 tablespoon salt
1 tablespoon chopped garlic
1 medium green bell pepper
1 tablespoon red pepper
1 (16-ounce) bottle of Italian salad dressing
1 cup melted margarine
1 (12-pound) wild turkey
5 gallons oil for frying

Purée onion, salt, garlic, bell pepper and red pepper in food processor. Add dressing and margarine; mix well. Inject marinade into turkey with syringe. Chill, covered, in refrigerator overnight. Heat oil in fish cooker. Add turkey. Cook for 1¼ hours or until turkey rises to top.

Yield: 12 to 15 servings

TURKEY CARIBE

8 turkey breast slices
4 slices American cheese, folded in half
¼ teaspoon garlic powder
¼ teaspoon onion powder
¼ teaspoon dried oregano leaves
8 slices bacon

Top each of 4 turkey slices with 1 slice cheese. Combine garlic powder, onion powder and oregano in bowl; mix well. Sprinkle over cheese. Top with remaining turkey slices. Wrap each with 2 slices bacon. Secure with wooden picks. Grill 6 inches from hot coals for 15 minutes, turning frequently.

Yield: 4 servings

GRILLED CATFISH

½ cup soy sauce
Juice of 1 lemon
1 tablespoon Worcestershire sauce
⅓ cup apple juice
2 cloves of garlic, minced
1 pound catfish fillets
Cinnamon to taste
Salt and pepper to taste

Combine soy sauce, lemon juice, Worcestershire sauce, apple juice and garlic in bowl; mix well. Add catfish. Marinate, covered, in refrigerator for 10 hours; drain. Place catfish in oiled wire broiler. Grill over medium coals for 10 minutes on each side. Sprinkle with cinnamon, salt and pepper.

Yield: 2 servings

SMOKEY CATFISH

1 (10-ounce) bottle of soy sauce
1 (10-ounce) bottle of Worcestershire sauce
10 drops of liquid smoke
3 pounds catfish fillets

Combine soy sauce, Worcestershire sauce and liquid smoke in bowl; mix well. Add catfish. Marinate, covered, in refrigerator for 2 hours. Heat coals and hickory chips in round smoker. Drain catfish. Place in smoker. Smoke for 2 hours or until fish flakes easily; do not overcook. Serve with butter-dill sauce and lemon wedges.

Yield: 6 servings

OUTDOOR LORE

Keep canned drinks cold in the washer by covering with ice. After the party, remove any remaining cans and spin water out.

GRILLED COD WITH DILL

1½ pounds cod fillets
1 cup tomato sauce
1 small onion, sliced
Salt and pepper to taste
2 teaspoons dillweed
3 tablespoons Parmesan cheese
½ green bell pepper, chopped
½ red bell pepper, chopped

Place fish on large sheet heavy-duty foil. Pour tomato sauce over top. Layer onion, salt, pepper, dillweed, Parmesan cheese and bell peppers over top. Seal foil. Place on grill. Cook over hot coals for 9 to 12 minutes or until fish flakes easily.

Yield: 4 servings

REDFISH WITH DIJON SAUCE

2 pounds redfish fillets
¼ cup apple juice
2 tablespoons lemon juice
Pepper to taste
Salt to taste
Garlic powder to taste
3 tablespoons each minced onion, margarine, Dijon mustard and apple juice
1 teaspoon basil or tarragon

Place fish in shallow bowl. Pour ¼ cup apple juice and lemon juice over fish. Marinate for 1 hour. Sprinkle with pepper, salt and garlic powder. Sauté onion in margarine in small saucepan until transparent. Add mustard, 3 tablespoons apple juice and basil; mix well. Cook until slightly thickened, stirring constantly. Place fish on perforated foil on grill. Grill over hot coals until fish flakes easily, basting frequently with sauce. Serve with remaining sauce.

Yield: 4 servings

HALIBUT IN FOIL

1 cup mayonnaise
1 cup sour cream
1 tablespoon dillweed
2½ to 3 pounds fresh halibut fillets

Combine mayonnaise, sour cream and dillweed in bowl; mix well. Spread mixture over halibut. Wrap in heavy foil. Cook on grill over hot coals for 20 minutes, turning once. Serve in foil. Garnish with parsley and lemon wedges.

Yield: 8 to 10 servings

FRESH SALMON

1 (2- to 3-pound) fresh salmon
2 or 3 slices bacon
Salt and pepper to taste

Pat salmon dry with paper towel. Place on large sheet heavy-duty foil. Arrange bacon diagonally over salmon. Season with salt and pepper. Seal foil tightly. Place on grill over hot coals. Cook for 30 to 45 minutes, turning every 10 minutes. Garnish with lemon wedges and parsley.

Yield: 8 to 10 servings

TERIYAKI SALMON STEAKS

1 cup teriyaki sauce
1 tablespoon peanut oil
3 tablespoons chopped parsley
1 clove of garlic, crushed
½ teaspoon freshly ground pepper
6 salmon steaks

Combine teriyaki sauce, peanut oil, parsley, garlic and pepper in bowl; mix well. Add salmon steaks. Chill for 1 to 2 hours, turning steaks every 20 to 30 minutes. Place steaks on sheet of heavy-duty foil. Grill for 4 to 5 minutes, basting with sauce. Turn steaks. Grill for 3 minutes or until fish flakes easily, basting with sauce. Serve hot or cold.

Yield: 6 servings

GRILLED SHARK STEAK

1½ cups unsalted butter
½ cup lemon juice
¼ cup finely chopped capers
⅓ teaspoon cayenne pepper
2 tablespoons teriyaki sauce
4 (8-ounce) shark steaks
Salt and pepper to taste

Heat butter in skillet for 10 minutes or until light brown, stirring frequently; do not burn. Add lemon juice, capers, cayenne pepper and teriyaki sauce; mix well. Remove from heat. Pat shark steaks dry with paper towel; season with salt and pepper to taste. Place in hinged fish basket sprayed with nonstick cooking spray. Place basket 6 inches from hot coals. Cook for 10 minutes, turning and basting with sauce every minute; do not overcook. Reheat remaining sauce. Serve with shark steaks.

Yield: 4 servings

GRILLED SNAPPER WITH LEMON

½ cup freshly squeezed lemon juice
1 teaspoon salt
½ teaspoon pepper
½ teaspoon thyme
1½ pounds snapper, sole or cod fillets
2 tablespoons melted butter

Combine lemon juice, salt, pepper and thyme in glass baking dish; mix well. Add fish; turn to coat. Chill, covered, for 1 hour, turning 3 times; drain. Brush with melted butter. Place on grill over hot coals. Grill for 5 minutes on each side or until fish flakes easily, turning once.

Yield: 4 servings

GRILLED SWORDFISH

1½ pounds swordfish steaks
3 tablespoons chopped green onions
2 tablespoons olive oil
1 tablespoon soy sauce
¼ teaspoon tarragon
¼ teaspoon basil
½ teaspoon chopped parsley
Juice and grated rind of 1 lemon

Place swordfish in lightly greased shallow dish. Sauté green onions in hot olive oil in skillet until tender. Add soy sauce, tarragon, basil, parsley, lemon juice and lemon rind; mix well. Simmer for 2 minutes. Pour over steaks. Marinate, covered, in refrigerator for 1 hour or longer. Grill 5 inches from heat source for 7 to 10 minutes on each side or until fish flakes easily.

Yield: 4 servings

GINGERY SWORDFISH STEAKS

2 tablespoons vegetable oil
2 tablespoons lemon juice
2 tablespoons low-sodium soy sauce
1 teaspoon grated lemon rind
1 tablespoon orange juice
2 cloves of garlic, minced
¼ teaspoon pepper
2 teaspoons minced fresh gingerroot
4 (4-ounce) swordfish steaks

Combine oil, lemon juice, soy sauce, lemon rind, orange juice, garlic, pepper and gingerroot in bowl; mix well. Arrange fish in shallow dish. Pour marinade over fish, turning to coat well. Marinate, covered, in refrigerator for 2 hours. Place on lightly greased grill 6 inches from hot coals. Broil for 6 minutes or until fish flakes easily, turning once. May substitute ¼ teaspoon ground ginger for fresh gingerroot.

Yield: 4 servings

SWEET-AND-SOUR SWORDFISH

12 ounces swordfish steaks
1 tablespoon vegetable oil
2 tablespoons red wine vinegar
1 tablespoon grated fresh gingerroot
1 tablespoon sugar
½ cup water
1½ teaspoons reduced-sodium soy sauce
1 cup chopped fresh pineapple
2 teaspoons cornstarch
3 tablespoons water
2 or 3 tablespoons chopped fresh cilantro
   leaves

Brush swordfish lightly with oil. Place on grill 6 inches above hot coals. Grill for 10 minutes per inch thickness or until fish flakes easily. Combine vinegar, gingerroot, sugar, ½ cup water, soy sauce and pineapple in small saucepan; mix well. Bring to a boil; reduce heat. Simmer for 2 minutes. Blend cornstarch with 3 tablespoons water in small bowl. Add to sauce. Cook just until thickened, stirring constantly. Spoon over swordfish; sprinkle with cilantro.

Yield: 2 servings

TANGY GRILLED FISH

2 pounds fish fillets
2 tablespoons olive oil
2 tablespoons lemon juice
2 tablespoons prepared horseradish
2 teaspoons prepared mustard
¼ teaspoon garlic powder
Paprika to taste

Brush fish with mixture of olive oil, lemon juice, horseradish, mustard and garlic powder; sprinkle with paprika. Grill over hot coals for 3 to 5 minutes. Turn fish and brush with remaining mixture. Grill until fish flakes easily. Serve with lemon wedges.

Yield: 5 servings

SMOKED TROUT

½ cup butter
1 teaspoon garlic powder
2 (2-pound) trout, cleaned
½ cup chopped almonds
1 lemon, cut into wedges

Melt butter in saucepan. Stir in garlic powder. Brush sauce over inside and outside of trout. Place in 9×13-inch foil baking pan. Sprinkle with almonds inside and outside. Arrange hot coals along outside edge of grill. Place pan on rack in center of grill. Close grill. Cook for 45 minutes to 1 hour or until fish flakes easily, basting with remaining sauce every 10 minutes. Serve with lemon wedges.

Yield: 4 to 6 servings

RAGIN' CAJUN SHRIMP

4 pounds shrimp, peeled
1 cup corn oil
½ cup chopped green onions
2 cloves of garlic, minced
1 teaspoon cayenne pepper
1 teaspoon black pepper
½ teaspoon crushed red pepper flakes
½ teaspoon thyme
½ teaspoon rosemary
¼ teaspoon oregano

Combine shrimp with corn oil, green onions, garlic, cayenne pepper, black pepper, red pepper flakes, thyme, rosemary and oregano in large bowl, stirring to coat shrimp. Refrigerate, covered, for 2 hours, stirring occasionally. Soak bamboo skewers in ice water for 2 hours. Preheat grill. Drain shrimp, reserving marinade. Thread shrimp on skewers. Grill just until pink, basting frequently with reserved marinade. Serve immediately.

Yield: 8 servings

LIME MARINATED SHRIMP

1½ pounds large shrimp, peeled
2 limes, cut into wedges
¾ cup fresh lime juice
1 tablespoon minced fresh ginger
2 small shallots, chopped
2 cloves of garlic, minced
1½ teaspoons lemon or lime marmalade
3 tablespoons finely chopped cilantro
½ teaspoon salt
⅛ teaspoon black pepper
⅛ teaspoon crushed red pepper flakes
⅓ cup olive oil
1 large cucumber, peeled, shredded
4 large carrots, peeled, shredded
1 head leaf lettuce, shredded
3 tablespoons finely chopped cilantro

Thread shrimp and lime wedges onto 4 skewers. Place in shallow glass dish. Combine next 9 ingredients in bowl. Whisk in olive oil gradually. Pour half the marinade over shrimp. Chill, covered, for 30 minutes, turning several times. Place cucumber, carrots, lettuce and 3 tablespoons cilantro on large platter. Pour remaining marinade over top, tossing lightly to coat well. Grill shrimp over medium heat for 5 minutes or just until cooked through, turning once. Place skewers on vegetable mixture. Serve immediately.

Yield: 4 servings

OUTDOOR LORE

Make your own Seasoned Salt for ourdoor cooking. Combine 1½ cups salt, 2 teaspoons marjoram, 2 tablespoons parsley flakes, 1 tablespoon garlic powder, 2 teaspoons curry powder, 2 teaspoons oregano, 1 teaspoon basil, 2 tablespoons onion powder, 1 teaspoon paprika, 2 tablespoons dry mustard, 2 tablespoons celery powder and 1 tablespoon MSG in covered jar; shake to mix. Store in tightly covered spice shakers.

SHRIMP AND CHICKEN KABOBS

1 bottle of Zesty Italian salad dressing
⅓ cup soy sauce
2 tablespoons lemon juice
1 clove of garlic
Shrimp, peeled
Boneless chicken, cut into pieces
Cherry tomatoes
Onions, cut into quarters
Green bell pepper, cut into pieces

Combine salad dressing, soy sauce, lemon juice and garlic in bowl; mix well. Thread shrimp, chicken, tomatoes, onions and green pepper alternately onto 8 skewers. Place in shallow dish. Pour marinade over kabobs. Marinate, covered, in refrigerator for 8 hours to overnight. Grill over hot coals for 4 minutes on each side.

Yield: 8 servings

SHRIMP AND SCALLOP KABOBS

1 (16-ounce) bottle of Catalina French dressing
2 tablespoons Worcestershire sauce
2 teaspoons garlic powder
2 teaspoons pepper
2 or 3 drops of Tabasco sauce
1 pound large shrimp, peeled
1 pound large scallops
1 large onion, cut into medium pieces

Combine salad dressing, Worcestershire sauce, garlic powder, pepper and Tabasco sauce in bowl; mix well. Place shrimp, scallops and onion in large dish. Pour marinade over all, covering completely. Marinate, covered, in refrigerator overnight. Drain, reserving marinade. Thread shrimp, scallops and onion onto skewers. Cover grill rack with foil; punch holes in foil with fork. Place skewers on foil. Cook, with lid down, over hot coals for 25 minutes or until shrimp and scallops are cooked through, turning and brushing occasionally with reserved marinade.

Yield: 6 servings

SPICY BARBECUE SAUCE

½ cup water
¼ cup soy sauce
2 tablespoons vinegar
1 cup catsup
1 tablespoon brown sugar
1 teaspoon prepared mustard
1 teaspoon prepared horseradish
⅛ teaspoon garlic powder
1½ teaspoons meat tenderizer

Combine water, soy sauce, vinegar, catsup, brown sugar, prepared mustard, horseradish, garlic powder and tenderizer in saucepan. Simmer for 10 to 15 minutes, stirring frequently. Use to baste steaks while grilling or cool and use as marinade.

Yield: 2 cups

SWEET BARBECUE SAUCE

2 to 3 tablespoons cornstarch
¼ cup packed brown sugar
1 cup sugar
1 teaspoon pepper
2 teaspoons prepared mustard
1 cup finely chopped onion
1 cup catsup
½ cup vinegar
¼ cup Worcestershire sauce
1 teaspoon Tabasco sauce
2 cups water

Combine cornstarch, brown sugar and sugar in saucepan. Add pepper, prepared mustard, onion, catsup, vinegar, Worcestershire sauce, Tabasco sauce and water; mix well. Bring to a boil, stirring constantly; reduce heat. Simmer for 30 minutes, stirring frequently. Delicious on chicken and hamburgers!

Yield: 1½ quarts

White Barbecue Sauce

1 cup mayonnaise
1 tablespoon lemon juice
1/4 cup vinegar
1 tablespoon sugar
1 tablespoon pepper

Combine all ingredients in bowl; mix well. Use for basting sauce for chicken while cooking on grill and also for sauce for cooked chicken.

Yield: 1 1/4 cups

Barbecue Sauce for 100

3 (32-ounce) bottles of Heinz catsup
1 1/4 cups lemon juice
1 1/4 cups Worcestershire sauce
1/4 cup plus 1 tablespoon liquid smoke
1/2 cup plus 2 tablespoons sugar
3 tablespoons celery seed
2 tablespoons chili powder

Combine catsup, lemon juice, Worcestershire sauce, liquid smoke, sugar, celery seed and chili powder in large saucepan. Simmer until of desired consistency. Use as sauce for 50 pounds cooked beef.

Yield: 100 servings

Peppery Barbecue Sauce

1 cup vinegar
1/2 cup water
1/2 cup margarine or oil
1 tablespoon crushed red pepper flakes
1 teaspoon black pepper
1 teaspoon salt

Combine vinegar, water, margarine and seasonings in saucepan. Bring to a boil. Boil for 5 minutes. Use to baste 1 whole chicken every 10 minutes while grilling, turning frequently. This takes a long time but it is worth the results.

Yield: 2 cups

Barbecue Sauce

6 tablespoons catsup
1/4 cup vinegar
2 tablespoons lemon juice
1/4 cup Worcestershire sauce
1/2 cup water
1/4 cup butter
6 tablespoons brown sugar
2 teaspoons salt
2 teaspoons dry mustard
2 teaspoons chili powder
2 teaspoons paprika
1 teaspoon cayenne pepper

Combine catsup, vinegar, lemon juice, Worcestershire sauce, water, butter, brown sugar, salt, dry mustard, chili powder, paprika and cayenne pepper in saucepan; mix well. Heat until well blended, stirring frequently. Use as desired.

Yield: enough for 5 to 6 pounds meat

Mr. David's Barbecue Sauce

4 cups vinegar
1 cup butter
2 tablespoons Worcestershire sauce
2 tablespoons chili powder
2 tablespoons Tabasco sauce
2 tablespoons paprika
3 tablespoons pepper
3 tablespoons salt
1 teaspoon dry mustard
1/2 teaspoon crushed red pepper flakes
2 cups catsup
1/2 cup lemon juice

Combine vinegar, butter, Worcestershire sauce, seasonings, catsup and lemon juice in large saucepan. Bring to a boil; reduce heat. Simmer for 30 minutes, stirring occasionally.

Yield: 8 cups

Easy Barbecue Sauce

1 (16-ounce) jar grape jelly
1 (32-ounce) bottle of catsup

Combine jelly and catsup in bowl; mix well. Use to baste chicken, pork or beef during last 5 minutes of cooking time. This sauce will burn easily.

Yield: 5 cups

Flip 'em Dip 'em Sauce

1 cup vegetable oil
1 cup margarine
2 cups white vinegar
1 tablespoon black pepper
2 tablespoons red pepper or red pepper flakes
1/4 cup (or less) salt

Combine all ingredients in saucepan; mix well. Bring to a boil. Marinate chicken in sauce before grilling. Dip 'em in sauce. Flip 'em and dip 'em when grilling. Decrease black and red pepper to taste.

*Yield: Enough for several chicken breasts or
2 whole chickens*

Club Marinade

1/2 cup orange juice
1/2 cup soy sauce
1 cup pineapple juice
1/4 cup sugar
1 clove of garlic, minced, or 1/4 teaspoon
   minced garlic

Combine orange juice, soy sauce, pineapple juice, sugar and garlic in medium bowl; mix well. Pour into shallow dish. Add steaks or boned chicken breasts. Marinate, covered, in refrigerator for 48 hours. Drain when ready to place on grill.

Yield: 2 cups

Jane's Grilling Marinade

1 small bottle of light soy sauce
1/4 cup lemon juice
1/2 cup butter
Dash of Worcestershire sauce
Dash of cayenne pepper

Combine soy sauce, lemon juice, butter, Worcestershire sauce and cayenne pepper in small saucepan. Heat until butter melts. Use to marinate chicken, pork chops or steak in refrigerator overnight and for basting while grilling.

Yield: 4 servings

Snappy Sauce

2 cups fresh lemon juice
2 cups catsup
3 tablespoons salt
2 ounces prepared mustard
3 cups Worcestershire sauce
2 cups vegetable oil
1/8 teaspoon Tabasco sauce

Combine all ingredients in bowl; mix well. Brush on meat while grilling and serve as side dish.

Yield: 6 1/2 cups

Teriyaki Marinade

1/2 cup soy sauce
1/4 cup packed brown sugar
2 tablespoons lemon juice
1/4 teaspoon dry ginger or 1/2 teaspoon fresh
   ginger
1 clove of garlic, minced

Combine soy sauce, brown sugar, lemon juice, ginger and garlic in bowl; mix well. Use to marinate beef, pork, poultry or fish for 1 hour or longer before grilling.

Yield: 3/4 cup

Outdoor Celebrations

When we think of outdoor celebrations, most of us come up with Fourth of July and Memorial Day, with maybe a smattering of summer birthdays thrown in for good measure. But with a little creative thinking, outdoor celebrations can take place any time the weather permits, and can mark anything from the end of the week to the end of a college career.

Did you ever consider making use of an outdoor grill to help prepare your Christmas feast? We did, and we've included some wonderful ideas to turn this traditional holiday into something really special.

Even something as formal and daunting, from a cook's point of view, as a wedding shower, can be adapted beautifully to an outdoor setting, as we show you in this chapter.

When it comes to summertime favorites, we've come up with a number of new suggestions to add sparkle, from a Fourth of July block party to fish fries, luaus and a family reunion menu to inspire the clan to gather every year.

Just let your imagination be your guide. After all, there's no reason why the setting for your next celebration shouldn't be as great as the great American outdoors.

GREAT EXPECTATIONS GRADUATION PARTY

Tortilla Pinwheels

Favorite Guacamole

Mexican Platter Dip

Assorted Chips   **Easy Coleslaw**

Spicy Fajitas   **Iron Skillet Casserole**

Corn Bread Casserole

Cheese Flan   **Burnt Milk Candy**

Citrus Cooler

Celebrate successful endings and bright beginnings outdoors fiesta-style. Colorful lanterns and flowers light up the night. Use baskets to make serving easy. There's enough of food for thought on this Tex-Mex menu to please everyone, regardless of age.

TORTILLA PINWHEELS

1 cup sour cream
1 can chopped green chiles
1 cup shredded Cheddar cheese
8 ounces cream cheese, softened
1 can chopped black olives
½ cup grated onion
Garlic powder and seasoned salt to taste
5 (10-inch) flour tortillas, softened

Combine fist 8 ingredients in bowl; mix well. Spread evenly over tortillas; roll as for jelly rolls. Wrap in plastic wrap. Chill for several hours. Slice into ½- to ¾-inch slices; arrange on serving plate with bowl of salsa in center.

Yield: 3 to 4 dozen

FAVORITE GUACAMOLE

4 or 5 avocados
2 tomatoes, finely chopped
1 teaspoon salt
1 tablespoon lemon juice
⅛ teaspoon garlic powder
1 teaspoon onion flakes
Tabasco sauce to taste

Cut avocados into halves lengthwise; remove and reserve seed. Scoop pulp into bowl; mash with fork, leaving slightly lumpy. Stir in remaining ingredients. Place avocado seed in dip to delay darkening. Chill, covered, for 2 to 3 hours. Remove seed. Serve with favorite tortilla chips. Store in covered container.

Yield: 10 to 12 servings

MEXICAN PLATTER DIP

2 (9-ounce) cans jalapeño bean dip
1 (8-ounce) carton avocado dip
1 cup sour cream
½ cup mayonnaise
2 tablespoons taco seasoning mix
⅓ cup sliced green onions
2 medium tomatoes, chopped
¾ cup sliced black olives
2 cups shredded mild Cheddar cheese

Spread jalapeño bean dip on 13-inch round platter. Spread avocado dip almost to edge of bean dip. Blend sour cream, mayonnaise and taco seasoning in bowl; spread almost to edge of avocado dip. Layer green onions, tomatoes, olives and cheese over top. Garnish around edge with alternating parsley sprigs and cherry tomatoes. Serve with nacho chips.

Yield: 8 to 10 servings

EASY COLESLAW

1 head cabbage, chopped
2 stalks celery, chopped
1 carrot, grated
½ onion, minced
1 to 1½ cups ranch salad dressing
Pepper to taste

Combine cabbage, celery, carrot, onion, salad dressing and pepper in bowl: mix well. Chill, covered, for several hours to overnight.

Yield: 6 to 8 servings

SPICY FAJITAS

1 (2-pound) flank steak
½ cup soy sauce
¼ cup Worcestershire sauce
½ cup teriyaki marinade
¼ cup orange juice
Seasoned salt, pepper and garlic powder
    to taste
2 cups shredded lettuce
2 cups chopped tomatoes
2 cups shredded Cheddar cheese
2 cups mashed avocado
2 cups hot refried beans
1 cup sour cream
1 cup picante sauce
12 (or more) flour tortillas

Pound steak with meat mallet. Marinate in mixture of soy sauce, Worcestershire sauce, teriyaki marinade, orange juice and seasonings in bowl overnight. Drain, reserving marinade. Grill over very low coals for 1 hour or until tender, turning and basting several times. Slice very thinly. Heat reserved marinade. Allow guests to assemble fajitas to their taste by placing steak and remaining ingredients on flour tortillas and rolling to enclose filling.

Yield: 12 servings

IRON SKILLET CASSEROLE

1 large onion, chopped
1 tablespoon vegetable oil
2 teaspoons garlic powder
1 pound ground beef
1 tablespoon sugar
1 teaspoon cumin
¼ teaspoon each salt and pepper
⅛ teaspoon cinnamon
1 (16-ounce) can whole tomatoes
2 (4-ounce) cans mild green chilies
1 (8-ounce) package tortilla chips
1 (6-ounce) can pitted black olives
2 cups shredded Cheddar cheese

Sauté onion in oil in cast-iron skillet. Add garlic powder and ground beef. Cook until ground beef is brown, stirring until crumbly. Add sugar and spices. Cook for 2 to 3 minutes longer, stirring constantly. Add undrained tomatoes and green chilies; mix well. Simmer for 10 minutes, stirring occasionally. Remove ground beef mixture to bowl. Wipe skillet with paper towel. Layer tortilla chips, ground beef mixture, olives and cheese ½ at a time in skillet. Bake at 400 degrees for 20 minutes.

Yield: 6 to 8 servings

CORN BREAD CASSEROLE

1 egg, beaten
1 cup sour cream
½ cup melted butter
1 (8-ounce) can cream-style corn
1 (8-ounce) can whole kernel corn
1 (8-ounce) package corn muffin mix

Combine first 5 ingredients in bowl; mix well. Stir in muffin mix. Pour into greased 9-inch square baking pan. Bake at 350 degrees for 40 minutes or until golden brown.

Yield: 6 servings

CHEESE FLAN

¼ cup (or more) sugar
1 (15-ounce) can sweetened condensed milk
1 (13-ounce) can evaporated milk
8 ounces cream cheese, softened
6 eggs

Caramelize sugar in top of double boiler or baking pan; tilt pan to coat side. Combine remaining ingredients in blender. Process for 1 minute or until smooth. Pour into prepared pan. Bake at 350 degrees for 20 minutes. Reduce temperature to 325 degrees. Bake for 1 hour longer. Chill, covered, overnight. Invert onto serving plate.

Yield: 8 to 10 servings

BURNT MILK CANDY

½ cup margarine
⅔ cup packed brown sugar
1 cup sweetened condensed milk
1 teaspoon vanilla extract
2 cups broken pecans, toasted

Microwave margarine in microwave-safe bowl for 1 minute or until melted. Blend in brown sugar and condensed milk. Microwave for 7 minutes, stirring every 2 minutes. Beat until stiff. Stir in vanilla and pecans. Spread in buttered 8-inch square dish. Chill until partially set. Cut into squares. Chill until firm.

Yield: 3 dozen

CITRUS COOLER

1 (46-ounce) can orange-pineapple juice
1 quart ginger ale

Chill juice and ginger ale. Mix in pitcher.

Yield: 6 to 8 servings

BACKYARD LUAU

Hawaiian Cheese Dip

Sweet-and-Sour Franks   **Shrimp Boil**

Hawaiian Baked Beans

Fruit Bread   **Fruit Pizza**

Tropical Sundaes or Melon Compote

Vanilla Wafer Cake

Pineapple Cooler

Theme parties are a hot trend and make party planning easy. Invitations, decorations, music and food all go Hawaiian, and guests dress the part for extra fun. Set a low table covered with a tropical print. Top with a layer of clear plastic and serve the Shrimp Boil right on the table.

HAWAIIAN CHEESE DIP

2 tablespoons melted margarine
8 ounces cream cheese, softened
3 cups shredded Cheddar cheese
¼ teaspoon garlic powder
½ cup snipped green onion tops
2 (4-ounce) cans chopped green chiles
1 cup cubed ham
1 round loaf Hawaiian bread

Combine first 7 ingredients in saucepan. Heat over low heat until cheeses melt, stirring occasionally. Scoop out center of loaf to form bowl; cut center into bite-sized pieces. Spoon dip into bread bowl. Serve with bread pieces. May wrap filled bread bowl in double-thickness heavy-duty foil. Keep warm over low coals on grill.

Yield: 10 to 12 servings

SWEET-AND-SOUR FRANKS

½ cup packed brown sugar
1 tablespoon cornstarch
⅓ cup red wine vinegar
⅓ cup chicken broth
¼ cup minced green bell pepper
2 tablespoons chopped pimento
1 tablespoon soy sauce
¼ teaspoon garlic powder
¼ teaspoon ginger
1 pound frankfurters

Combine brown sugar and cornstarch in saucepan. Blend in vinegar and chicken broth. Add green pepper, pimento, soy sauce, garlic powder and ginger. Cook over medium heat until thick and bubbly, stirring constantly. Cut frankfurters into bite-sized pieces. Add to sauce. Heat to serving temperature.

Yield: 10 servings

SHRIMP BOIL

6 onions, cut into quarters
6 lemons, cut into quarters
Red and black pepper to taste
1 package shrimp and crab boil
3 pounds small new potatoes
12 ears of corn, cut into 2-inch pieces
5 pounds fresh shrimp in shell
¼ cup salt (optional)

Bring a generous amount of water with onions, lemons, pepper and shrimp and crab boil to a boil in large stockpot on stove or grill. Add potatoes. Boil for 15 minutes. Add corn. Boil for 5 minutes. Add shrimp. Boil for 7 minutes. Add salt; remove from heat. Let stand, covered, for 5 minutes. Remove shrimp and vegetables with wire basket.

Yield: 6 to 8 servings

HAWAIIAN BAKED BEANS

2 (16-ounce) cans pork and beans in
   tomato sauce
2 (15-ounce) cans three bean salad, drained
2 (8-ounce) cans juice-pack crushed
   pineapple, drained
⅔ cup spicy barbecue sauce
½ cup packed brown sugar
2 tablespoons Worcestershire sauce
4 ounces ham, chopped

Combine all ingredients in 3-quart casserole; mix well. Bake, uncovered, at 350 degrees for 1 hour or until bubbly; mix well.

Yield: 12 servings

FRUIT BREAD

3 cups sugar
1 cup vegetable oil
4 eggs
1 teaspoon each cinnamon and nutmeg
1½ teaspoons salt
2 teaspoons baking soda
3½ cups flour
⅔ cup water
2 cups mashed bananas
1½ cups chopped nuts

Combine sugar and oil in bowl. Add eggs; mix well. Add sifted dry ingredients alternately with water. Add bananas and nuts; mix well. Pour into 2 greased 5×9-inch loaf pans. Bake at 350 degrees for 70 minutes. May bake in 7 greased 16-ounce cans until loaves test done.

Yield: 2 large or 7 small loaves

Pumpkin Bread: Substitute pumpkin for bananas. **Applesauce Bread:** Substitute applesauce for bananas and ⅔ cup cider for water. **Orange Bread:** Substitute unpeeled ground oranges for bananas and orange juice for water.

Fruit Pizza

1 package refrigerator sugar cookie dough
8 ounces cream cheese, softened
1 (7-ounce) jar marshmallow creme
Assorted bite-size fresh fruit
1 jar strawberry glaze

Slice cookie dough; arrange on 14-inch pizza pan and press to form crust. Bake at 350 degrees for 10 to 14 minutes or until golden brown. Cool. Blend cream cheese and marshmallow creme in bowl. Spread over cookie crust. Arrange concentric circles of fruit such as strawberries, pineapple, kiwifruit, raspberries and blueberries over top. Drizzle glaze over fruit using decorating tube. Cut into wedges.

Yield: 8 to 16 servings

Tropical Sundaes

3 nectarines
6 plums
3 kiwifruit, peeled
2 cups strawberries
2 tablespoons lime juice
2 quarts lime or rainbow sherbet
¼ cup coarsely chopped macadamia nuts

Cut fruit into bite-size pieces; combine in bowl. Sprinkle with lime juice. Chill in refrigerator. Scoop sherbet into serving dishes. Top with fruit and nuts.

Yield: 8 to 10 servings

Outdoor Lore

For a Pineapple Cooler, fill tall glasses with pineapple sherbet. Add orange soda and garnish with pineapple slices and sprigs of mint.

Melon Compote

1 small watermelon
1 honeydew melon
1 cantaloupe
½ cup frozen orange juice concentrate,
    thawed
2 tablespoons fresh lime juice
2 cups fresh pineapple chunks, chilled
½ cup flaked coconut

Cut slice from watermelon rind lengthwise to form flat base. Cut top ⅓ from watermelon in zigzag pattern. Scoop pulp from watermelon to form bowl. Cut pulp into balls. Cut honeydew and cantaloupe into balls. Combine melon pieces in large bowl. Add orange juice concentrate and lime juice; mix gently until coated. Chill melon and melon shell in refrigerator. Place melon balls and pineapple in melon bowl. Sprinkle with coconut. Garnish with mint sprigs.

Yield: 15 servings

Vanilla Wafer Cake

2 cups sugar
1 cup margarine, softened
6 eggs
1 (12- to 15-ounce) package vanilla wafers,
    crushed
½ cup milk
1 medium package flaked coconut
1½ cups nuts

Cream sugar and margarine in mixer bowl until light and fluffy. Beat in eggs 1 at a time. Add vanilla wafer crumbs and milk; mix well. Add coconut and nuts; mix well. Spoon into greased tube pan. Bake at 275 degrees for 2 hours.

Yield: 16 servings

OLD-FASHIONED ICE CREAM CRANKING

Lemon Velvet Ice Cream

Country-Style Ice Cream

Peanut Butter Ice Cream

Pineapple Cheesecake

Chocolate Cake

Almost Mrs. Field's Cookies

Invite everyone to bring a freezer full of homemade ice cream and have a tasting party. Add a buffet of favorite toppings and desserts. New-Fashioned flavors celebrate any summer occasion.

LEMON VELVET ICE CREAM

5⅓ cups each whipping cream and milk
Juice of 8 lemons
4 cups sugar
2 teaspoons lemon extract
1 tablespoon grated lemon rind

Combine all ingredients in large bowl; mix well. Pour into ice cream freezer container. Freeze using manufacturer's instructions.

Yield: 3 quarts

COUNTRY-STYLE ICE CREAM

2¼ cups sugar
4 eggs, beaten
4 cups each whipping cream and milk
2 tablespoons vanilla extract
½ teaspoon salt

Add sugar to eggs in bowl gradually, beating until thickened. Stir in remaining ingredients. Pour into ice cream freezer container. Freeze using manufacturer's instructions.

Yield: 1 gallon

PEANUT BUTTER ICE CREAM

2 cups sugar
6 eggs
1½ cups chunky peanut butter
1 (15-ounce) can sweetened condensed milk
2 (12-ounce) cans evaporated milk
1 quart milk
2 tablespoons vanilla extract

Beat sugar and eggs in mixer bowl until thick. Add peanut butter; beat well. Blend in remaining ingredients. Pour into ice cream freezer container. Freeze using manufacturer's instructions.

Yield: 10 to 12 servings

PINEAPPLE CHEESECAKE

1 (3-ounce) package lemon gelatin
1 cup boiling water
1½ cups graham cracker crumbs
½ cup melted margarine
1 cup sugar
8 ounces cream cheese, softened
1¾ cups whipping cream, whipped
1 cup drained crushed pineapple

Dissolve gelatin in boiling water in bowl. Cool. Mix crumbs and margarine in bowl. Press into 8×10-inch dish. Cream sugar and cream cheese in bowl until light and fluffy. Fold in whipped cream gently. Fold in pineapple. Pour into prepared dish. Garnish with additional crumbs. Chill for 2 hours or until set.

Yield: 12 servings

CHOCOLATE CAKE

2 cups sugar
¾ cup shortening
½ cup baking cocoa
1 teaspoon salt
2 teaspoons baking soda
2 eggs
1 cup buttermilk
1 teaspoon vanilla extract
2½ cups flour
1 cup boiling water

Combine first 5 ingredients in mixer bowl; beat until well mixed. Beat in eggs, buttermilk and vanilla. Add flour; mix well. Add boiling water; mix well. Pour into greased 9×13-inch cake pan. Bake at 350 degrees for 30 to 35 minutes or until cake tests done; do not overbake.

Yield: 16 servings

ALMOST MRS. FIELD'S COOKIES

2 cups butter, softened
2 cups sugar
2 cups packed brown sugar
4 eggs
2 teaspoons vanilla extract
4 cups flour
1 teaspoon salt
5 cups rolled oats, pulverized in blender
2 teaspoons baking powder
2 teaspoons baking soda
3 cups chocolate chips
1 (8-ounce) milk chocolate bar, grated
1 cup chopped nuts

Cream butter, sugar and brown sugar in mixer bowl until light and fluffy. Add eggs and vanilla; mix well. Add mixture of flour, salt, oats, baking powder and baking soda; mix well. Stir in chocolate chips, grated chocolate and nuts. Shape into balls; place 2 inches apart on cookie sheet. Bake at 375 degrees for 6 minutes.

Yield: 9 to 10 dozen

RED, WHITE AND BLUE BASH

Firecracker Franks

Red, White and Blue Salads

Spiced Patties on Buns

Chicken Casserole

Sorghum Main Dish Beans

Crazy Sam's Garlic Slaw

Make-Ahead Potato Salad

Microwave Mud Brownies

Cheesecake

Dirt Cake

Close off the streets, set up the grills, and turn on the fireworks for a block-buster neighborhood block party. Kids of all ages enjoy the all-American menu and a star-spangled good time.

FIRECRACKER FRANKS

1 cup catsup
1 cup packed brown sugar
½ cup grape jelly
¼ to ½ cup chicken broth
¼ teaspoon dry mustard
1 pound frankfurters

Combine first 5 ingredients in saucepan or fondue pot. Simmer for 5 minutes, stirring occasionally. Cut frankfurters into bite-size pieces. Add to catsup mixture. Simmer until heated through.

Yield: 10 servings

STRAWBERRY PRETZEL SALAD

2 cups coarsely crushed pretzels
¾ cup melted margarine
2 tablespoons sugar
8 ounces cream cheese, softened
8 ounces whipped topping
½ cup sugar
1 large package strawberry gelatin
2 cups boiling water
2 (10-ounce) packages frozen strawberries

Combine pretzels, margarine and 2 tablespoons sugar in bowl; mix well. Press into 9×13-inch baking dish. Bake at 400 degrees for 8 minutes. Cool. Beat cream cheese, whipped topping and ½ cup sugar in mixer bowl until well blended. Spread over cooled crust. Dissolve gelatin in boiling water in heatproof bowl. Add frozen strawberries; stir until thawed. Spoon over cream cheese mixture. Chill until firm.

Yield: 15 servings

BLUEBERRY SALAD

1 large package grape gelatin
2 cups boiling water
1 large can crushed pineapple
1 can blueberry pie filling
8 ounces cream cheese, softened
1 cup sour cream
½ cup sugar
1 teaspoon vanilla extract

Dissolve gelatin in boiling water in heatproof bowl. Stir in pineapple and pie filling. Pour into serving dish. Chill until firm. Combine cream cheese, sour cream, sugar and vanilla in mixer bowl; beat until smooth and creamy. Spread over gelatin layer. Chill until serving time.

Yield: 10 servings

SPICED PATTIES

1 cup soft bread crumbs
½ cup milk
1 egg, beaten
1 pound ground beef
1 teaspoon salt
⅛ teaspoon allspice

Soak crumbs in milk in bowl for several minutes. Add egg, ground beef and seasonings; mix lightly. Shape into patties. Place on grill over hot coals. Grill for 15 minutes or until done to taste, turning once.

Yield: 4 servings

CHICKEN CASSEROLE

4 to 6 chicken breasts, cooked
1 package chicken-flavored Rice-A-Roni
½ cup chopped celery
½ cup chopped onion
½ cup chopped green bell pepper
1 small jar chopped pimento
1 can sliced water chestnuts
2 cans cream of mushroom soup
1 can mushrooms
1 cup shredded sharp Cheddar cheese
15 to 20 butter crackers, crushed
½ cup melted margarine

Cut chicken into bite-size pieces. Cook Rice-A-Roni using package directions. Combine chicken, Rice-A-Roni, celery, onion, green pepper, pimento, water chestnuts, soup and mushrooms in large bowl; mix well. Spoon into buttered 9×13-inch baking dish. Toss cheese, cracker crumbs and margarine in bowl; sprinkle over casserole. Bake at 400 degrees for 20 minutes or until brown.

Yield: 8 servings

SORGHUM MAIN DISH BEANS

4 slices bacon, chopped
1 onion, chopped
1 pound ground beef
½ cup pure sorghum molasses
½ cup catsup
3 tablespoons vinegar
1 tablespoon prepared mustard
1 (16-ounce) can pork and beans
1 (16-ounce) can lima beans
1 (16-ounce) can kidney beans

Cook bacon and onion with ground beef in skillet until ground beef is brown and crumbly, stirring frequently. Stir in molasses, catsup, vinegar and mustard. Mix in undrained beans. Spoon into 9×13-inch baking dish. Bake at 350 degrees for 1½ hours.

Yield: 16 to 20 servings

CRAZY SAM'S GARLIC SLAW

1 medium head cabbage, shredded
8 green onions, finely chopped
1 cup mayonnaise
4 teaspoons vinegar
1 teaspoon each garlic powder and salt
½ teaspoon pepper

Combine cabbage and remaining ingredients in large bowl; mix well. Chill, covered, for 2 hours.

Yield: 10 servings

MAKE-AHEAD POTATO SALAD

1½ cups mayonnaise
1 cup sour cream
1½ teaspoons horseradish
1 teaspoon celery seed
½ teaspoon salt
1 cup freshly chopped parsley
2 medium onions, chopped
8 medium potatoes, cooked

Combine mayonnaise, sour cream, horseradish, celery seed and salt in bowl; mix well and set aside. Mix parsley and onions in bowl; set aside. Peel potatoes; cut into ⅛-inch slices. Layer potatoes, mayonnaise mixture and parsley mixture alternately in large salad bowl, ending with parsley mixture; do not stir. Chill, covered, for 8 hours or longer.

Yield: 8 to 10 servings

MICROWAVE MUD BROWNIES

½ cup butter
1 cup sugar
2 eggs, slightly beaten
¾ cup flour
⅛ teaspoon salt
¼ cup baking cocoa
1 teaspoon vanilla extract
½ cup chopped pecans
1½ cups miniature marshmallows
¼ cup butter, softened
3 tablespoons milk
3 tablespoons baking cocoa
½ teaspoon vanilla extract
2 cups sifted confectioners' sugar

Microwave ½ cup butter in microwave-safe bowl until melted. Add sugar and eggs; mix well. Add mixture of flour, salt and ¼ cup baking cocoa; mix well. Stir in 1 teaspoon vanilla and pecans. Spread in greased 8-inch square microwave-safe baking dish. Microwave on Medium for 6 to 7 minutes, turning once. Microwave on High for 2 to 3 minutes. Sprinkle marshmallows over top. Cover with foil. Let stand for 2 minutes. Combine ¼ cup butter, milk, 3 tablespoons baking cocoa, ½ teaspoon vanilla and confectioners' sugar in bowl; beat until creamy. Spread over brownies. Cool completely. Cut into squares.

Yield: 16 servings

CHEESECAKE

12 graham crackers, crushed
¼ cup melted butter
24 ounces cream cheese, softened
5 eggs
1 cup sugar
2 teaspoons vanilla extract
2 cups sour cream
6 tablespoons sugar
2 teaspoons vanilla extract

Mix cracker crumbs and butter in bowl. Press over bottom of 9×13-inch baking dish. Combine cream cheese, eggs, 1 cup sugar and 2 teaspoons vanilla in mixer bowl; beat until creamy. Pour into prepared dish. Blend sour cream, 6 tablespoons sugar and 2 teaspoons vanilla in bowl. Pour over cream cheese mixture. Bake at 300 degrees for 45 to 50 minutes or until firm.

Yield: 16 servings

DIRT CAKE

8 ounces cream cheese, softened
¼ cup butter or margarine, softened
½ to 1 cup confectioners' sugar
2 small packages vanilla instant pudding mix
3 to 3½ cups cold milk
12 ounces whipped topping
1 large package Oreo cookies, crushed

Combine first 3 ingredients in bowl; beat until creamy. Prepare pudding mix with milk using package directions. Add pudding and whipped topping to cream cheese mixture; mix well. Alternate layers of cookie crumbs and cream cheese mixture in new 1-gallon plastic flowerpot, beginning and ending with crumbs. Place bouquet of red, white and blue silk flowers in pot and attach toy shovel. Chill or freeze until serving time. Use shovel to serve. May also layer half the cookie crumbs, all the cream cheese mixture and remaining crumbs in 9×13-inch dish. May use poinsettias for Christmas.

Yield: 25 servings

TGIF POOL PARTY

Dried Beef Dip

Antipasto

Lettuce Salad

Sausage-Chicken Kabobs

Pool Party Shrimp

Grilled Rice Casserole

Grilled Onions

Strawberry Delight

Caramel Fondue

Celebrate the weekend with an early evening dip and feast. There's nothing here to heat up the kitchen—the preparation's done in the refrigerator or on the grill. Set up two grills—one for the entrées and one for the veggies. Roll a wheelbarrow filled with ice for the drinks and salad to a likely spot and relax—it's Friday!

DRIED BEEF DIP

16 ounces cream cheese, softened
1 (8-ounce) jar dried beef, chopped
1 (12-ounce) can Ro-Tel tomatoes
1 bunch green onions, chopped

Combine cream cheese, dried beef, tomatoes and green onions in bowl; mix well. Chill, covered, in refrigerator. Serve with corn chips.

Yield: 8 servings

ANTIPASTO

Flowerets of 1 head cauliflower
1 green bell pepper, cut into strips
1 large carrot, sliced
4 stalks celery, sliced
1 (7-ounce) jar pickled sour onions
8 ounces button mushrooms
2 cloves of garlic, pressed
1½ cups wine vinegar
½ cup vegetable oil
⅓ cup sugar
2 teaspoons prepared mustard
2 teaspoons salt
1 teaspoon oregano leaves

Combine vegetables and garlic in large bowl. Pour mixture of vinegar, oil, sugar, mustard, salt and oregano over vegetables. Chill, covered, for 12 hours or longer, turning vegetables over occasionally. Drain well; arrange vegetables on serving plate. Garnish with black olives and pimentos.

Yield: 8 to 10 servings

LETTUCE SALAD

1 head lettuce
2 or 3 hard-boiled eggs, chopped
Sweet salad pickle cubes
Salt and pepper to taste
Mayonnaise to taste

Tear lettuce; place in salad bowl. Add eggs. Add desired amounts of pickle cubes, salt and pepper and mayonnaise; toss salad.

Yield: 6 servings

OUTDOOR LORE

For insect-proof serving outdoors, stretch plastic wrap in various-size embroidery hoops. Use as covers over salads or other dishes. Food is protected and guests can see what's inside.

SAUSAGE-CHICKEN KABOBS

⅔ cup teriyaki sauce
⅔ cup orange juice
6 tablespoons sugar
6 tablespoons vegetable oil
8 chicken breast filets, cut into chunks
1 (8-ounce) package brown-and-serve sausages
1 (8-ounce) can pineapple chunks, drained

Combine teriyaki sauce, orange juice, sugar and oil in bowl. Add chicken; toss lightly to coat. Chill for 30 minutes. Drain, reserving marinade. Cut sausages into halves. Thread chicken, sausages and pineapple alternately onto 14-inch skewers. Grill or broil for 10 to 12 minutes or until chicken is tender, basting frequently with reserved marinade and turning once.

Yield: 8 servings

POOL PARTY SHRIMP

3 pounds fresh shrimp, peeled
⅔ cup melted butter
¼ cup finely chopped onion
¼ cup chili sauce
½ teaspoon garlic salt
Dash of Tabasco sauce
⅓ cup chopped parsley
2 tablespoons freshly squeezed lemon juice
Dash of Worcestershire sauce

Cut six 12-inch squares heavy-duty foil. Place shrimp on foil. Combine butter, onion, chili sauce, garlic salt, Tabasco sauce, parsley, lemon juice and Worcestershire sauce in bowl; mix well. Spoon about 3 tablespoonfuls over each shrimp portion. Seal foil, making double folds. Place foil packets on grill 4 inches above hot coals. Cook for 20 minutes or until shrimp are pink.

Yield: 6 servings

GRILLED RICE CASSEROLE

1 pound sausage
1 bunch green onions, chopped
3 stalks celery, finely chopped
¼ cup butter
Salt and pepper to taste
1 can sliced water chestnuts
1 jar sliced mushrooms
1 envelope chicken noodle soup mix
1 (6-ounce) package long grain and
    wild rice mix
2½ cups water
1 (3-ounce) package slivered almonds

Brown sausage in skillet, stirring until crumbly; drain. Sauté green onions and celery in butter in skillet until tender. Combine with sausage, salt, pepper and next 5 ingredients in 9×12-inch casserole; mix well. Top with almonds. Place on side of grill. Turn other side of grill to Medium. Bake for 35 to 40 minutes or until rice is tender.

Yield: 6 servings

GRILLED ONIONS

4 large Vidalia onions, peeled, rinsed
4 teaspoons butter
4 beef bouillon cubes
Salt and pepper to taste

Remove onion cores. Place each onion on foil folded to a double thickness. Place 1 teaspoon butter and 1 bouillon cube in center of each. Sprinkle with salt and pepper; seal foil. Grill for 45 minutes.

Yield: 4 servings

STRAWBERRY DELIGHT

1 cup flour
¼ cup packed brown sugar
⅔ cup pecans
½ cup butter
2 egg whites
⅔ cup sugar
10 ounces whipped topping
1 (10-ounce) package frozen strawberries,
    thawed
1 tablespoon lemon juice

Combine flour, brown sugar and pecans in bowl; mix well. Cut in butter until mixture is crumbly. Spread on baking sheet. Bake at 325 degrees for 20 minutes. Cool and crumble. Spread ⅔ of the mixture in 9×13-inch baking dish. Beat egg whites in mixer bowl until stiff peaks form. Fold sugar, whipped topping, strawberries and lemon juice into egg whites in bowl. Spoon into prepared dish. Top with remaining crumbs. Freeze, covered, for 3 hours or longer.

Yield: 15 servings

CARAMEL FONDUE

1 (16-ounce) package caramels
½ cup milk
1 (4-ounce) package chopped pecans
Bite-size fresh fruit

Combine caramels and milk in saucepan. Cook over low heat until caramels are melted, stirring frequently. Add pecans; mix well. Pour into cooking bag; seal. Heat bag in boiling water on grill. Serve with assorted fresh fruit for dipping or pour over fruit.

Yield: 10 to 15 servings

OUTDOOR WEDDING RECEPTION

Tea Sandwiches

Decorated Mints

Mixed Nuts

Wedding Cake

Red Velvet Groom's Cake

Delta Mint Tea

Few celebrations are as joyous as a wedding, and a beautiful spot outdoors with Mother Nature as the decorator is the perfect place to have a party afterwards. Gather garden flowers to adorn everything— tables, cake plates and serving pieces.

TEA SANDWICHES

24 ounces cream cheese, softened
1 bunch green onions, chopped
1 can chopped black olives
1 small can mushrooms, drained, chopped
1 jar dried beef, chopped
1 tablespoon MSG
1 loaf very thinly sliced white bread

Combine cream cheese, green onions, olives, mushrooms, dried beef and MSG in bowl; mix well. Trim crusts from bread. Flatten with rolling pin. Spread half the bread with cream cheese mixture; top with remaining bread. Cut into decorative shapes.

Yield: 3 to 4 dozen

RED VELVET GROOM'S CAKE

2½ cups sifted flour
1½ cups sugar
1 teaspoon each baking soda and baking cocoa
1 cup buttermilk
1½ cups vegetable oil
1 teaspoon white vinegar
2 eggs
1 teaspoon each butternut and vanilla extract
1 (1-ounce) bottle of red food coloring
½ cup margarine
8 ounces cream cheese, softened
½ teaspoon vanilla extract
1 (1-pound) package confectioners' sugar
1 cup toasted chopped pecans

Sift flour, sugar, baking soda and cocoa into bowl. Add next 7 ingredients, mixing well after each addition. Pour into 3 greased and floured 8-inch cake pans. Bake at 350 degrees for 30 minutes or until cake tests done. Cream margarine and cream cheese in mixer bowl until light. Add ½ teaspoon vanilla and confectioners' sugar; beat until creamy. Stir in pecans. Spread between layers and over top and side of cake. Place small vial in top of cake to hold fresh flowers. Decorate edge of cake plate with flowers.

Yield: 16 servings

DELTA MINT TEA

7 tea bags
12 sprigs of fresh mint
Peeled rind of 3 lemons
8 cups boiling water
Juice of 7 lemons and/or oranges
2 cups sugar
8 cups cold water

Steep tea bags, mint and lemon rind in boiling water in large container for 12 minutes. Discard tea bags, mint and rind. Add juice and sugar; mix until sugar dissolves. Strain into large pitcher. Add cold water.

Yield: 1 gallon

SEASIDE BUFFET

Two-Cheese Ball

Vegetable Marinade Supreme

Barbecued Prawns

Fried Fish Fillets

Tangy Coleslaw

Creamy Potato Bake

Cheesy Bread Kabobs

Whether your shoreline is on the ocean, river bank or poolside, this seafood dinner is a winner. Everything can be made ahead or cooked on the grill for an easy party. The stars and the sand are free.

TWO-CHEESE BALL

16 ounces cream cheese, softened
10 ounces sharp Cheddar cheese, shredded
2 tablespoons chopped green onions
2 teaspoons Worcestershire sauce
1 (8-ounce) can crushed pineapple, drained
⅔ cup chopped pecans

Combine cream cheese, Cheddar cheese, green onions and Worcestershire sauce in bowl; mix well. Add pineapple; mix well. Chill, covered, for several hours. Shape into ball; roll in pecans. Chill, covered, until serving time. Serve with assorted crackers.

Yield: 12 servings

VEGETABLE MARINADE SUPREME

1 red bell pepper
1 green bell pepper
3 cucumbers
1 bunch broccoli
½ head cauliflower
½ cup tarragon vinegar
1 tablespoon lemon juice
¼ teaspoon garlic powder
1 tablespoon dry mustard
1 tablespoon Dijon mustard
¼ teaspoon pepper
¼ cup sugar
⅓ cup olive oil
½ cup freshly chopped parsley

Cut vegetables into bite-sized pieces. Combine in large bowl; toss lightly. Combine vinegar and remaining ingredients in bowl; mix well. Pour over vegetables. Marinate, tightly covered, in refrigerator for 24 hours. Garnish with cherry tomatoes and ripe olives.

Yield: 8 to 10 servings

BARBECUED PRAWNS

1 pound prawns in shells
½ cup soy sauce
2 tablespoons orange juice
2 tablespoons sugar

Soak wooden skewers in cold water for 30 minutes. Rinse prawns; drain. Pull legs; do not remove shells. Thread onto wooden skewers. Heat soy sauce, orange juice and sugar in large flat pan until simmering. Simmer for 1 minute. Grill prawns on skewers over hot coals for 1 minute. Dip into heated sauce to coat; return to grill. Grill for 1 minute on each side. Repeat dipping and grilling 2 or 3 times. Dip prawns into sauce; arrange skewers on serving plate. Garnish with lemon wedges.

Yield: 4 servings

Fried Fish Fillets

3 to 4 pounds thick firm white fish fillets
1 tablespoon salt
3 cups yellow cornmeal
¼ cup flour
1 tablespoon seasoned salt
1½ teaspoons garlic powder
Vegetable oil for deep-frying

Place fish in large bowl. Add salt and enough water to cover. Chill for 2 to 3 hours. Drain; pat dry. Combine next 4 ingredients in plastic bag. Add fish 1 piece at time; shake to coat. Place fillets in 350-degree hot oil. Deep-fry for 5 minutes or until fillets rise to surface, turning occasionally. Drain on paper towels. Serve immediately.

Yield: 12 servings

Tangy Coleslaw

1 head cabbage, shredded
1 onion, sliced
1 green bell pepper, sliced
1 teaspoon salt
¾ cup sugar
¼ cup vegetable oil
6 tablespoons white vinegar

Place vegetables in large container; sprinkle with salt. Combine sugar, oil and vinegar in saucepan. Bring to a boil. Boil for 1 minute. Cool. Pour over vegetables; toss to coat. Store, tightly covered, in refrigerator for up to 1 week.

Yield: 8 servings

Outdoor Lore

For a new wrinkle on toasted marshmallows, fill doughnut hole with marshmallow. Thread stick through doughnut and marshmallow. Toast over low coals until marshmallow is soft.

Creamy Potato Bake

5 medium potatoes
1 medium onion, sliced
6 tablespoons butter
⅓ cup shredded Cheddar cheese
2 tablespoons chopped parsley
1 tablespoon Worcestershire sauce
Salt and pepper to taste
⅓ cup chicken broth

Peel and slice potatoes. Place potatoes and onion on 18×22-inch piece heavy-duty foil. Dot with butter. Sprinkle with cheese, parsley, Worcestershire and salt and pepper. Fold edges up; add broth. Seal foil tightly. Grill over medium-hot coals in covered grill for 35 minutes or until potatoes are tender.

Yield: 6 servings

Cheesy Bread Kabobs

1 (5-ounce) jar sharp American cheese spread
1 tablespoon butter, softened
1 tablespoon sliced green onions
¼ teaspoon tarragon
½ teaspoon parsley flakes
Garlic powder to taste
8 slices French bread

Combine cheese, butter, green onions, tarragon, parsley and garlic powder in bowl; mix well. Make two 4-layer sandwiches with bread, spreading cheese mixture between layers and over top and bottom. Cut each sandwich into quarters. Thread each quarter onto skewer. Grill over medium coals for 6 to 7 minutes or until lightly toasted, turning frequently.

Yield: 8 servings

SPECIAL HOLIDAY DINNER

Christmas Cheese Ball

Pâté Supreme

Spinach Salad

Cornish Hens with Stuffing

Holiday Baked Beans

**No-Bake Fruitcake or
Orange Pound Cake**

Candy Cane Ice Cream

Cookie Jar Gingersnaps

Spiced Apple Cider

Whether you're fortunate enough to be able to enjoy the holidays out of doors or simply use the grill as an extra kitchen, this elegant menu will give everyone reason to celebrate the Christmas spirit.

CHRISTMAS CHEESE BALL

*16 ounces cream cheese, softened
1 small can crushed pineapple, drained
¼ cup chopped green bell pepper
1 tablespoon minced onion
1 tablespoon seasoned salt
Chopped pecans*

Mix first 5 ingredients in bowl. Shape into ball; roll in pecans. Chill until serving time.

Yield: 12 servings

PÂTÉ SUPREME

*4 ounces thin-sliced bacon
1 tablespoon each chopped onion and parsley
8 ounces calves liver, cut into small pieces
1 egg yolk
1 cup each bread crumbs and beef consommé
Salt and pepper to taste*

Line 2-cup mold with 3 strips bacon; place in refrigerator. Cut remaining bacon into small pieces. Fry bacon in skillet for 5 minutes. Add onion, parsley and liver. Cook for 5 minutes or until brown. Cool. Process mixture in blender. Add egg yolk; mix well. Combine crumbs and consommé in bowl. Let stand for several minutes. Add to liver mixture; mix well. Add salt and pepper. Pack into prepared mold. Place mold in large pan of hot water. Bake at 300 degrees for 2 hours. Unmold onto plate.

Yield: 8 servings

SPINACH SALAD

*1 pound spinach, torn
1 medium head romaine, torn
Segments of 1 large pink grapefruit
Segments of 1 large orange
1 large avocado, sliced
1 small red onion, sliced
½ cup salted roasted peanuts
½ cup vegetable oil
¼ cup cider vinegar
1 teaspoon grated orange rind
1 teaspoon sugar
¼ cup orange juice
1 clove of garlic, pressed
1 tablespoon minced parsley
½ teaspoon each curry powder, ginger, pepper and paprika*

Layer first 7 ingredients in salad bowl. Combine oil and remaining ingredients in bowl; mix well. Pour over salad; toss to mix. Serve immediately or chill until serving time.

Yield: 8 to 10 servings

CORNISH HENS WITH STUFFING

1 (6-ounce) package long grain and wild rice
  mix, cooked
¼ cup golden raisins
2 tablespoons butter
2 tablespoons slivered blanched almonds
4 (1- to 1½-pound) Cornish hens
Salt to taste
¼ cup melted butter

Mix first 4 ingredients in bowl. Rub Cornish hen cavities with salt. Spoon ¾ cup rice mixture into each hen; truss. Brush with melted butter; place in foil pan. Arrange medium-hot coals around edge of grill; place pan on grill in center, leaving space between hens. Grill for 1½ hours or until tender, brushing occasionally with pan drippings.

Yield: 4 servings

HOLIDAY BAKED BEANS

1 cup chopped onion
1 tablespoon vegetable oil
1 (32-ounce) can pork and beans
1 cup packed dark brown sugar
1 pound bacon, crisp-fried, crumbled
½ cup each mustard and catsup
¼ cup Worcestershire sauce

Sauté onion in skillet in oil until tender. Combine with remaining ingredients in large bowl. Spoon into baking dish. Bake at 350 degrees for 1½ hours.

Yield: 10 servings

NO-BAKE FRUITCAKE

1 large package marshmallows
1 (15 ounce) can sweetened condensed milk
1 package graham cracker crumbs
1½ pounds chopped pecans
1 pound chopped English walnuts
1½ pounds candied cherries, chopped
1½ pounds candied pineapple, chopped

Heat marshmallows in condensed milk in large heavy saucepan over low heat until marshmallows melt; remove from heat. Stir in crumbs. Pour over mixture of nuts and candied fruit in large bowl; mix well with buttered hands. Pack into buttered tube pan; cover with buttered waxed paper. Chill in refrigerator for 1 week. Turn onto serving plate.

Yield: 30 servings

ORANGE POUND CAKE

¼ cup butter
½ cup chopped pecans
1 cup (or more) sliced candied cherries
8 egg whites
1 cup sugar
1 pound butter, softened
2 cups sugar
8 egg yolks
2 teaspoons vanilla extract
2 teaspoons almond extract
1 teaspoon butternut extract
3 cups sifted flour
⅓ cup orange juice

Grease and flour 10-inch tube pan. Dot bottom of pan with ¼ cup butter; sprinkle pecans and candied cherries over bottom. Beat egg whites in mixer bowl until stiff peaks form. Add 1 cup sugar gradually, beating constantly until stiff. Set aside. Cream 1 pound butter with 2 cups sugar in mixer bowl until light and fluffy. Beat in egg yolks 1 at a time. Stir in flavorings. Add flour alternately with orange juice, beating well after each addition and beginning and ending with flour. Fold in egg whites gently. Spoon into prepared pan. Bake at 350 degrees for 1½ hours or until cake tests done. Cool in pan on wire rack. Invert onto serving plate.

Yield: 16 servings

CANDY CANE ICE CREAM

1½ cups crushed peppermint candy
4 cups half-and-half
4 eggs
1 cup sugar
2 tablespoons vanilla extract
1 teaspoon oil of peppermint
4 cups whipping cream
½ teaspoon salt
1 to 2 cups milk
1½ cups crushed peppermint candy

Combine first 2 ingredients in bowl. Let stand for several hours. Beat eggs in mixer bowl until foamy. Add sugar; beat until thick and lemon-colored. Add next 4 ingredients; beat until blended. Pour into 1-gallon ice cream freezer. Add candy and half-and-half mixture. Add milk to fill-line. Freeze using manufacturer's instructions for 10 minutes or until partially frozen. Add crushed candy. Freeze for 10 minutes longer.

Yield: 8 to 10 servings

COOKIE JAR GINGERSNAPS

¾ cup shortening
1 cup sugar
1 egg
¼ cup molasses
2 cups sifted flour
1 tablespoon ginger
2 teaspoons baking soda
1 teaspoon cinnamon
½ teaspoon salt
Sugar

Beat shortening and 1 cup sugar in mixer bowl until creamy. Beat in egg and molasses. Sift in next 5 ingredients; mix well. Shape by teaspoonfuls into balls; roll in sugar. Place 2 inches apart on ungreased cookie sheet. Bake at 350 degrees for 12 to 15 minutes or until crackly and brown. Cool on wire rack. Store in airtight container.

Yield: 3 dozen

SPICED APPLE CIDER

2 quarts apple cider
1½ quarts cranberry juice cocktail
¼ cup packed brown sugar
1¼ teaspoons whole cloves
3 cinnamon sticks
1 lemon, thinly sliced

Combine apple cider, cranberry juice cocktail and brown sugar in 40-cup coffee maker. Place spices and lemon in basket. Perk using manufacturer's instructions.

Yield: 32 servings

PLAYHOUSE WARMING

Roll-Up Sandwiches

Carrot and Celery Sticks

Potato Chips

Ice Cream Cones

Orange Juice

Welcome tiny friends to share a new playhouse with this finger-food lunch. Invite the dolls and Teddy bears too—everyone loves to celebrate moving into a new house.

ROLL-UP SANDWICHES

Trim crusts from bread. Flatten each slice with rolling pin. Spread with mixture of peanut butter and jelly or with cheese spread. Roll up as for jelly roll. Chill, covered, in refrigerator.

FAMILY REUNION

A gathering of generations is cause for celebrating—a time to reminisce, to catch up on what's new, and to sample the family's favorite dishes. Just set the food out on a long table, and don't worry about a menu. Scatter hay bales covered with quilts around the yard for extra seating. Watching children play and story telling keep everyone entertained.

HOMEMADE PIMENTO CHEESE

16 ounces extra-sharp Cheddar cheese, shredded
1 (4-ounce) jar chopped pimento
⅓ cup (or more) mayonnaise

Combine all ingredients in large bowl; mix well. Pack into crock. Serve with wheat crackers.

Yield: 4 cups

BAKED CHICKEN NUGGETS

7 or 8 boned whole chicken breasts
2 cups fine dry bread crumbs
1 cup Parmesan cheese
1½ teaspoons salt
1 tablespoon fresh or 1 teaspoon dried thyme
1 tablespoon fresh or 1 teaspoon dried basil
1 cup melted butter

Cut chicken into 1½-inch pieces. Combine bread crumbs, cheese and seasonings in shallow dish. Dip chicken into butter in bowl; coat with crumb mixture. Place in single layer on baking sheet. Bake at 400 degrees for 30 minutes.

Yield: 3 dozen

DILL GARLIC PICKLES

1 gallon dill pickles, drained
1 (5-pound) package sugar
6 to 8 cloves of garlic, minced
½ teaspoon Tabasco sauce

Cut pickles crosswise into 1- to 1½-inch chunks. Place in large bowl. Add remaining ingredients; mix well. Let stand until sugar is dissolved, stirring occasionally. Return to jar. Store in refrigerator.

Yield: 1 gallon

SQUASH RELISH

12 cups finely chopped squash
4 cups chopped onions
2 cups each chopped green and red bell pepper
3 or 4 hot red peppers, chopped
2½ cups vinegar
2 tablespoons salt
5 cups sugar
3 tablespoons turmeric
1 tablespoon each mustard seed and pepper

Mix all ingredients in stockpot. Cook over medium heat for 35 to 40 minutes or until thick, stirring frequently. Pour into hot sterilized jars, leaving ½-inch headspace; seal with 2-piece lids.

Yield: 8 pints

PATIO TUNA SALAD

1 can cream of shrimp soup
2 cups cooked macaroni
1 (7-ounce) can tuna, drained, flaked
½ cup chopped green bell pepper
2 tablespoons sliced stuffed olives
1 tablespoon finely chopped onion
1 tablespoon lemon juice
Dash of pepper

Combine all ingredients in bowl; mix well. Chill until serving time. Serve on crisp greens.

Yield: 4 to 8 servings

GOLDEN PASTA SALAD

1 pound rotelle pasta
2 cups mayonnaise
1 cup sugar
½ cup vinegar
½ teaspoon turmeric
Salt and pepper to taste
1 cup water
1 cup chopped celery
½ to ¾ cup grated carrots
1 onion, chopped

Cook pasta using package directions; drain. Place in serving bowl. Let stand until cool. Combine mayonnaise, sugar, vinegar, turmeric, salt and pepper in bowl; mix well. Stir in water, celery, carrots and onion. Add to cooled pasta; toss gently. Chill, covered, overnight.

Yield: 6 to 8 servings

BROCCOLI SALAD

Flowerets of 2 bunches broccoli
¾ cup raisins
10 slices crisp-fried bacon, crumbled
½ cup sugar
2 tablespoons cider vinegar
1 cup mayonnaise-type salad dressing
½ teaspoon salt
½ cup finely chopped onion

Combine broccoli, raisins and crumbled bacon in large bowl. Combine sugar, cider vinegar, mayonnaise-type salad dressing, salt and onion in bowl; mix well. Add to broccoli mixture; mix well. Chill, covered, until serving time.

Yield: 8 servings

SWEET-AND-SOUR CHICKEN

6 chicken breasts
1 envelope dry onion soup mix
1 (8-ounce) jar apricot preserves
1 (8-ounce) jar Russian salad dressing

Place chicken breasts in baking dish. Pour mixture of remaining ingredients over chicken. Bake at 350 degrees for 45 minutes to 1 hour or until chicken is tender. Serve over rice, noodles or veggies.

Yield: 6 servings

CHICKEN SPAGHETTI

1 medium green bell pepper, chopped
1 medium onion, chopped
½ cup margarine
1 chicken, cooked, chopped
1 can mushrooms, drained
1 can tomato soup
1 can cream of chicken soup
8 to 12 ounces spaghetti, cooked
1 cup shredded Cheddar cheese

Sauté green pepper and onion in margarine in large skillet. Add chicken, mushrooms and soups; mix well. Simmer for 20 minutes. Place enough spaghetti in 9×13-inch baking dish to fill half full. Pour chicken mixture over spaghetti. Top with cheese. Bake at 350 degrees for 30 minutes.

Yield: 10 servings

FANNIE SUE'S MEAT LOAF

1 medium onion, chopped
4 slices white bread, shredded
2 pounds lean ground beef
1 egg, slightly beaten
½ teaspoon salt
Pepper to taste
½ cup water
2 (8-ounce) cans tomato sauce
1 tablespoon prepared mustard
¼ cup sugar
¼ cup water

Combine onion, bread, ground beef, egg, salt, pepper, ½ cup water and ½ can tomato sauce in bowl; mix well. Pat into cast-iron skillet. Bake at 350 degrees for 40 minutes; drain. Pour mixture of 1½ cans tomato sauce and remaining ingredients over meat loaf. Bake for 20 minutes longer. Let stand for 10 minutes before serving.

Yield: 6 to 8 servings

CABBAGE CASSEROLE

1 medium head cabbage, cut into wedges
¼ cup melted butter
¼ cup flour
½ teaspoon salt
¼ teaspoon pepper
2 cups milk
1 small green bell pepper, chopped
1 medium onion, chopped
1 cup shredded Cheddar cheese
½ cup mayonnaise

Cook cabbage in boiling salted water in saucepan until tender; drain. Arrange in 9×13-inch casserole. Combine butter and flour in saucepan; mix well. Heat until bubbly. Stir in ½ teaspoon salt, pepper and milk. Cook over medium heat until thickened, stirring constantly. Pour over cabbage. Bake at 375 degrees for 20 minutes. Spread mixture of remaining ingredients over top. Bake at 400 degrees for 20 minutes.

Yield: 8 to 10 servings

POTATO CASSEROLE

1 (2-pound) package frozen hashed brown
   potatoes
½ cup chopped onion
½ cup melted margarine
1 teaspoon salt
¼ teaspoon pepper
1 cup sour cream
1 can cream of chicken soup
10 ounces Cheddar cheese, shredded
2 cups cornflakes, crushed
¼ cup melted margarine

Combine hashed brown potatoes, onion, ½ cup margarine, salt, pepper, sour cream, soup and Cheddar cheese in bowl; mix well. Spoon into greased 9×13-inch baking dish. Sprinkle mixture of cornflakes and ¼ cup margarine over top. Bake at 350 degrees for 45 minutes or until bubbly.

Yield: 8 servings

COUNTRY POTATOES

1 (2-pound) package frozen potatoes, thawed
1 teaspoon salt
¼ teaspoon pepper
½ cup melted butter
1 can cream of chicken soup
1 cup sour cream
10 ounces Cheddar cheese, shredded
2 cups crushed cornflakes
¼ cup melted butter

Combine potatoes, salt, pepper, ½ cup butter, soup, sour cream and Cheddar cheese in bowl; mix well. Spoon into lightly greased 9×13-inch baking dish. Top with mixture of cornflakes and ¼ cup melted butter. Bake at 350 degrees for 45 minutes.

Yield: 8 servings

WILD RICE

2 tablespoons chopped onion
1 (4-ounce) can mushrooms, drained
2 tablespoons margarine
1 package long grain and wild rice
1 tablespoon Kitchen Bouquet
2 tablespoons catsup
1 teaspoon Worcestershire sauce
2½ cups water
1 cup sour cream

Sauté onion and mushrooms in margarine in saucepan. Add remaining ingredients except sour cream; mix well. Bring to a boil; reduce heat. Simmer for 25 minutes. Stir in sour cream just before serving.

Yield: 6 servings

SPUDNUTS

1 cup margarine, softened
¾ cup sugar
1½ cups mashed potatoes
1½ cups lukewarm milk
1¼ teaspoons salt
2 tablespoons dry yeast
½ cup lukewarm water
3 eggs, beaten
8 cups flour

Cream margarine, sugar and mashed potatoes in mixer bowl until light and fluffy. Add milk and salt; mix well. Dissolve yeast in warm water. Stir into potato mixture. Add eggs; beat well. Stir in flour gradually. Knead on floured surface until smooth. Place in greased bowl, turning to grease surface. Let rise until doubled in bulk. Knead until smooth. Roll out on floured surface. Cut with doughnut cutter. Let rise for 1 hour. Deep-fry several at a time in hot oil until golden brown. Drain on paper towel.

Yield: 3½ dozen

GRANDMA'S COCONUT CAKE

1 (2-layer) package yellow cake mix
3 eggs
½ cup butter, softened
1 (3-ounce) package vanilla instant
    pudding mix
1⅓ cups water
1 cup sour cream
2 cups sugar
4¼ cups frozen flaked coconut, thawed

Prepare cake mix using package directions with eggs, butter, pudding mix and water. Pour into 3 greased and floured 9-inch round cake pans. Bake at 350 degrees for 25 minutes. Remove to wire rack to cool. Combine sour cream, sugar and 2¼ cups coconut in bowl; mix well. Chill, covered, for 3 hours. Spread between layers and over top and side of cake. Sprinkle with remaining 2 cups coconut. Chill, covered, for 2 days.

Yield: 12 servings

TURTLE CAKE

1 (2-layer) package German chocolate cake
    mix, batter prepared
½ cup margarine
1 (10-ounce) package caramels
½ (15-ounce) can sweetened condensed milk
1 cup chocolate chips
1 cup chopped pecans

Pour half the batter into greased 9×13-inch cake pan. Bake at 350 degrees for 15 minutes. Melt margarine and caramels in double boiler over hot water, stirring frequently; remove from heat. Blend in condensed milk. Sprinkle chocolate chips and pecans over baked layer. Drizzle caramel mixture over all. Top with remaining cake batter. Bake for 25 minutes longer.

Yield: 20 servings

BUTTERMILK CAKE

3 cups cake flour
1 teaspoon baking soda
¼ teaspoon salt
1 cup shortening
2 cups sugar
4 eggs
1 teaspoon vanilla extract
1 cup buttermilk
½ cup butter, softened
½ cup milk
2 cups sugar
1 teaspoon vanilla extract

Sift flour, baking soda and salt together. Cream shortening and 2 cups sugar in mixer bowl until light and fluffy. Add eggs and 1 teaspoon vanilla; mix well. Add buttermilk alternately with flour mixture a small amount at a time, beating until smooth after each addition. Pour into greased and floured tube pan. Bake at 350 degrees for 55 minutes or until cake tests done. Cool in pan for 10 minutes. Turn onto wire rack to cool completely. Combine remaining ingredients in saucepan. Boil for 1 minute. Beat until thickened. Drizzle over cake.

Yield: 12 servings

EGG CUSTARD PIE

4 eggs, well beaten
2 cups milk
1 cup sugar
1 teaspoon vanilla extract
Pinch of salt
1 unbaked (9-inch) deep-dish pie shell

Combine eggs, milk, sugar, vanilla and salt in bowl; mix well. Pour into pie shell. Bake at 425 degrees for 35 to 40 minutes or until set.

Yield: 6 servings

PUMPKIN CAKE

2 cups sugar
1 (16-ounce) can pumpkin
1 cup vegetable oil
4 eggs, beaten
2 cups flour
1 teaspoon salt
2 teaspoons baking soda
2 teaspoons baking powder
2 teaspoons cinnamon
½ cup flaked coconut
½ cup chopped pecans
Cream Cheese Frosting

Combine sugar, pumpkin, oil and eggs in mixer bowl. Beat at medium speed for 1 minute. Add mixture of flour, salt, baking soda, baking powder and cinnamon. Beat for 1 minute. Stir in coconut and pecans. Pour into 3 greased and floured 8-inch round cake pans. Bake at 350 degrees for 25 minutes or until cake tests done. Cool in pans for 10 minutes. Remove to wire rack to cool completely. Frost with Cream Cheese Frosting.

Yield: 12 servings

CREAM CHEESE FROSTING

½ cup butter, softened
8 ounces cream cheese, softened
1 (1-pound) package confectioners' sugar
2 teaspoons vanilla extract
½ cup chopped pecans
½ cup flaked coconut

Cream butter and cream cheese in mixer bowl until light and fluffy. Add confectioners' sugar and vanilla; beat until creamy. Stir in pecans and coconut.

Yield: 4 cups

Outdoor Essentials

Whether you wear the outdoor chef's hat in the fully equipped kitchen of an RV or while hovering over a fire with nothing but green sticks and aluminum foil, you can turn out delicious food using the recipes and ideas in this cookbook.

Just in case you need a refresher course in some of the specific techniques for outdoor cookery, we've gathered how-to's for everything from building the fire to cooking an entire meal at once in a Dutch oven tower. You'll find diagrams for making perfect foil packets, mix-and-match kabob ideas, how to grill vegetables, and one-pot meal recipes for over a week's worth of menus from easy, basic ingredients.

While you're planning your foray into the great outdoors, take time to make sure you leave the outdoors "great." Pack a reusable basket or container with permanent dishes and utensils. Use cloth napkins and tablecloths instead of paper products. Recycle plastic bottles to carry beverages. Separate trash into bags or containers for cans, paper, glass, etc., to take home for recycling.

The best part of cooking—and eating—outdoors is the chance to appreciate your natural environment. Notice everything, protect what needs protecting, and leave only your footsteps behind you.

LIGHTING YOUR FIRE

- Start charcoal fire with bed of briquettes 2 to 3 inches deep about 30 to 40 minutes before cooking. Make your own fire starters by placing briquettes in egg cartons. Pour melted paraffin over briquettes. Place on top of unlighted briquettes.

- Heat coals to the specified temperature.

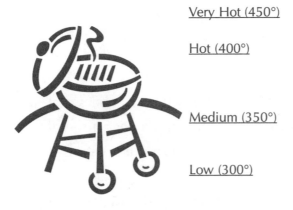

<u>Very Hot (450°)</u>	Coals will be glowing with gray ash on edges.
<u>Hot (400°)</u>	Coals will be covered with gray ash. You will be able to hold your hand 4 inches from heat source for 2 seconds.
<u>Medium (350°)</u>	You will be able to hold your hand 4 inches from heat source for 4 seconds.
<u>Low (300°)</u>	You will be able to hold your hand 4 inches from heat source for 5 seconds.

Add flavor and zip to your coals by adding wood chips, nuts or herbs. The smoke adds a subtle flavor.

- Mesquite chips add lively flavor to chicken and beef.

- Apple and peach fruitwoods add a sweet accent to pork and poultry.

- Hickory and maple add a smoky taste to pork, ham or poultry.

- Cracked nuts in the shell add subtle flavor.

- Fresh or dried herbs scattered on the coals add distinctive taste.

- Soak wood chips, nuts or herbs in cold water for 30 minutes before using.

DUTCH OVEN COOKING

A Dutch oven is ideal for camping because so many recipes may be baked or cooked in one. Dutch ovens may be stacked to cook several dishes at once.

- Preheat charcoal briquettes for 30 minutes before using. Spread evenly on ground and set Dutch oven in coals. Pile an equal number of coals on lid with more toward the edge than in the center. Use more coals on top on cold or windy days.

- Use a number of briquettes equal to two times the diameter of the oven for moderate heat. Use coals equal to three times the diameter for high heat.

- Almost any food such as stews, pot roasts, beans and vegetables may be cooked in about the same amount of time as on the stove or in the oven.

- Bake biscuits, corn bread and cakes according to package directions.

COOKING ON SKEWERS

Almost any food—fruits, vegetables, meats, poultry or seafood—can be grilled on skewers. Easy to prepare ahead to the point of grilling, these meals on a stick are extra fast to cook. Just marinate the meat and precook vegetables for several minutes before assembling. Leave a small space between items. Grill on greased rack over hot coals for 8 to 10 minutes. Choose any combination from these suggestions. Let everyone do his own.

- *Meat*
  - Shrimp, shelled
  - Scallops
  - Tuna, swordfish, catfish or fillets, cut into 1-inch pieces
  - Boneless chicken breasts, cut into 1-inch pieces
  - Boneless lamb, beef sirloin or lean pork, cut into 1-inch pieces
  - Kielbasa or other sausages, cut into 1-inch pieces
  - Cooked ham cubes

- *Fruit*
  - Apple wedges
  - Papaya, peeled, cut into 1-inch pieces
  - Orange sections
  - Fresh or canned pineapple cubes

- *Vegetables* (precooked)
  - Summer squash
  - Broccoli flowerets
  - Cauliflowerets
  - Fresh corn, cut into 1-inch pieces
  - New potatoes, cut into halves
  - Carrots, cut into chunks

Outdoor Essentials

FOIL PACKET COOKING

Cooking in aluminum foil is clean and easy, and there are no pots to carry or dishes to wash. Aluminum foil is used to broil, braise, sauté and steam foods. Steaming, the most common method, is done by sealing the food in foil so that moisture cannot escape.

Be patient when cooking in foil over coals. Allow the flames to die down until the coals are all gray. Spread the coals out to make a layer 1 coal deep; place food packets on coals. Cooking time will depend on how hot the fire is. (Coals are very hot, and you don't need a lot to cook a dinner completely.)

Steps in Sealing Food in Aluminum Foil

1. Cut a piece of foil that will be large enough to make your seal. If you are using single weight, have piece large enough to fold in half for double thickness. A good idea is to cut one piece first and check on size before you cut pieces for your total needs. Do not skimp on the amount of aluminum foil you use to make your seal.

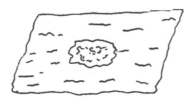  

2. Place food in center of foil, shiny side up.

3. Bring sides of foil up over the food loosely. Fold the top ½ inch down on itself. This can be creased.

4. Fold the top down again on itself. Do not crease.

5. Fold the top down flat. Also press the ends together.

6. Fold corners over, along the dotted lines. Fold pointed ends over, about ½ inch, along dotted lines.

7. Fold ends over again. This is now ready to go on the hot coals.

GRILLING FROM THE GARDEN

Any vegetable can be grilled in foil packets. However, most vegetables can be placed directly on grill. Rinse, trim and precook vegetables if necessary. Brush with olive oil or melted margarine. Cook over medium coals until slightly charred and tender.

Use grilled vegetables as an addition to pasta salads, to top pizza or hamburgers, to stir into cooked vegetables or baked beans, and to spice up spaghetti sauce, sandwiches or pitas.

Timings for Grilled Vegetables

Vegetables	Preparation	Precooking time	Grilling time
Asparagus	Snap off and discard tough bases of stems.	3 to 4 minutes	3 to 5 minutes
Fresh baby carrots	Cut off carrot tops. Wash and peel.	3 to 5 minutes	3 to 5 minutes
Corn	Leave husk on.	Do not precook.	15 to 20 minutes
Eggplant	Cut off top and blossom ends. Cut eggplant crosswise into 1-inch-thick slices.	Do not precook.	8 minutes
Green or red bell peppers	Remove stem. Cut peppers into quarters; cut into 1-inch-wide strips.	Do not precook.	8 to 10 minutes
New potatoes	Cut potatoes into halves.	10 minutes or until almost tender.	10 to 12 minutes
Zucchini	Wash; cut off ends. Quarter lengthwise into long strips.	Do not precook.	5 to 6 minutes
Baby squash	Rinse and trim ends.	Precook whole for 3 minutes.	20 minutes
Tomatoes	Cut into quarters.	Do not precook.	20 minutes

MASTERFUL ONE-POT MEALS

Put into one pot: 3 pounds ground beef (browned and drained)
2 or 3 chopped onions
1 or 2 chopped green bell peppers
2 cans undiluted tomato soup

Add your choice of ingredients and cook over hot coals for 15 minutes.

American Chop Suey
Omit tomato soup
Add:
four 20-ounce cans spaghetti

Spanish Rice
Add:
one 15-ounce package minute rice, cooked

Mac Beef
Add:
one 2-pound package macaroni, cooked

Hunter's Stew
Add:
4 cans undiluted vegetable soup

Yaki Special
Add:
3 pounds canned spaghetti
2 pounds canned peas, drained

Speedy Chili
Add:
4 pounds canned kidney beans, drained
Chili powder to taste

Squaw Corn
Add:
3 pounds canned corn, drained
8 ounces cheese, cubed

Hungarian Hot Pot
Add:
4 pounds baked beans

Ranch Beans
Omit tomato soup
Add:
2 cups catsup
2 envelopes onion soup mix
two 28-ounce cans baked beans

Chicken Mac
Omit tomato soup
Add:
2 cans chicken gumbo soup
2 cans cream of chicken soup
2 soup cans water
When boiling add:
1 pound uncooked macaroni
Cook covered.

Campfire Soup
Omit onions and green peppers
Add:
6 soup cans water
2 envelopes onion soup mix
2 tablespoons soy sauce
1 teaspoon oregano
2 cups sliced carrots
2 cups sliced celery
Cook covered.

Chili Pie
Add:
one 16-ounce can Mexicorn
one 7-ounce can pitted olives
1 can tomato soup
When boiling add:
one 15-ounce package corn bread mix prepared as directed and dropped by spoonfuls.
Cook covered.
DO NOT LIFT COVER!

Accompaniments
Cornfetti, 25
Dill Garlic Pickles, 110
Pickled Mushrooms, 15
Squash Relish, 110

Appetizers. *See also* Dips; Snacks;
    Spreads
Antipasto, 102
Cheese Balls with Olives, 60
Chinese Chicken Wings, 57
Fruit Kabobs, 19
Pigs in Mufflers, 11
Potted Franks, 22
Pumpernickel Bites, 22
Sausage Balls, 17
Sesame-Cheese Bites, 25
Speedy Chicken Wings, 12
Stuffed Mushrooms, 14
Supreme Pâté, 107
Tortilla Pinwheels, 92

Apples
Apples and Crumbles, 53
Applesauce Bread, 95
Applesauce Spice Cake, 53
Camper's Apples, 29
Nutty Apple Crisp, 57
Slow-Cooker Apples, 18

Beans
Baked Beans, 59
Barbecued Beans, 64
Bean and Celery Bake, 49
Bean Casserole, 49
Beany Weeny, 42
Calico Beans, 26
Hawaiian Baked Beans, 95
Holiday Baked Beans, 108
Sorghum Main Dish Beans, 100
Three-Bean Bake, 49

Beef. *See also* Ground Beef
Barbecued Beef Brisket, 70
Barbecued Beef Short Ribs, 72
Basic Marinated Steak, 68
Beach Steak Sandwich, 37
Beef Alamo, 68
Beef and Bacon Twirls, 56
Beef Kabobs, 72

Beef Stroganoff, 36
Campfire Stew, 36
Cornish Pastries, 14
Dutch Oven Beef Stew, 36
Eggs in Bologna, 48
English Beef Rib Barbecue, 71
Famous Shish Kabobs, 73
Fiesta Beef Kabobs, 73
Foil Packet Hobo Dinner, 74
Gingery Flank Steak, 69
Grilled London Broil, 70
Grilled Rib-Eye Steaks, 68
Grilled Sirloin Tip, 71
Grilled Steak, 69
Grilled Tenderloin, 70
Korean Sirloin Skewers, 72
Lemony Chuck Roast, 36
Marinated Chuck Roast, 69
Marinated Kabobs, 72
Marinated Roast Sirloin, 71
Marinated Round Steak, 71
Meal in a Packet, 69
Mexican Kabobs, 73
Sirloin Kabobs, 74
Spicy Fajitas, 93
Steak Roll Broil, 68
Steak Strips en Brochette, 74
Tailgate Barbecue, 25
Teriyaki Kabobs, 74
Teriyaki Pinwheels, 67
Teriyaki Steak, 70

Beverages
Banana Shake, 29
Citrus Cooler, 94
Delta Mint Tea, 104
Four-Fruit Punch, 21
Grape Juice Fizzy, 11
Lemonade Tea Punch, 26
Orange Julius, 57
Peppermint-Orange Sipper, 11
Pineapple Cooler, 96
Spiced Apple Cider, 109

Breads. *See also* Muffins; Pancakes
Applesauce Bread, 95
Camper's Coffee Cake, 51
Campfire Corn Cakes, 52
Cheesy Bread Kabobs, 106
Cheesy French Bread, 35

Index

Index

Corn Light Bread, 26
Dutch Oven-Baked Bread, 31
French Toast Crunch, 29
Fruit Bread, 95
Frying Pan Bread, 51
Grilled French Bread, 64
Italian Cheese Ring, 57
Orange Bread, 95
Pumpkin Bread, 95
Slim Jim Breadsticks, 8
Stromboli Bread, 9
Swiss Cheese Bread, 23
Tonka Toast, 52

Cakes. *See also* Frostings
Applesauce Spice Cake, 53
Buttermilk Cake, 114
Campfire Cupcakes, 35
Carrot-Walnut Cake, 16
Chocolate Cake, 98
Fresh Apple Cake, 24
Grandma's Coconut Cake, 113
In-a-Jiffy Cake, 61
Orange Pound Cake, 108
Pineapple Cake, 54
Poppy Seed Cake, 64
Pumpkin Cake, 114
Red Velvet Groom's Cake, 104
Stuck-in-the-Mud Cake, 13
Turtle Cake, 113
Upside-Down Cake, 31
Vanilla Wafer Cake, 96

Candy
Burnt Milk Candy, 94
Peanut Clusters, 24
Pecan Oatmeal Chewies, 9

Chicken
Baked Chicken Nuggets, 110
Barbecued Chicken, 43, 80
Boneless Chicken Breasts, 61
Cafe-Style Barbecue Chicken, 79
Chicken and Stuffing, 44
Chicken Barbecue, 80
Chicken Breast Marinade, 80
Chicken Cacciatore, 63
Chicken Casserole, 99
Chicken Dinner in Foil, 45
Chicken-in-the-Garden, 34

Chicken Kabobs, 81
Chicken Liver Kabobs, 81
Chicken Spaghetti, 111
Chicken with Mushrooms, 43
Chicken Yogurt Kabobs, 81
Chinese Chicken Wings, 57
Cold Broiled Chicken, 9
Easy Barbecued Chicken, 79
Flowerpot Chicken, 44
Foiled Chicken, 44
Greek Chicken, 79
Grilled Chicken, 44
Grilled Chicken Marinade, 80
Lemon-Garlic Chicken, 82
Lemon-Pepper Chicken, 82
Low-Cal Chicken, 67
Make-Ahead Chicken, 79
Marinated Grilled Chicken, 81
Mexican Chicken, 82
Minted Chicken, 82
Onion-Barbecued Chicken, 45
Orange Jubilee Chicken, 20
Oriental Chicken Pitas, 20
Outdoor Chicken Divan, 45
Peanut Chicken Skewers, 83
Sausage-Chicken Kabobs, 102
Shrimp and Chicken Kabobs, 88
Skillet Chicken, 45
Speedy Chicken Wings, 12
Sweet-and-Sour Chicken, 111
Teriyaki Chicken, 82

Chili
Brunswick Chili, 63
Devil's Delight Chili, 37

Coleslaw
Barbecue Slaw, 66
Celery Seed Slaw, 25
Crazy Sam's Garlic Slaw, 100
Easy Coleslaw, 93
German Coleslaw, 22
Oklahoma Cabbage Slaw, 62
Tangy Coleslaw, 106

Cookies. *See also* Cookies, Bar
Almost Mrs. Field's Cookies, 98
Cookie Jar Gingersnaps, 109
Glorified Shortbread, 14
Treasure Pops, 10

Cookies, Bar
Best-Ever Brownies, 59
It's-a-Lemon Bars, 13
Microwave Mud
  Brownies, 100
Yummy Bars, 9

Corn
Barbecued Corn, 50
Corn Bread Casserole, 93
Corn in Husks, 50
Corn-on-the-Cob, 35
Corny Stew, 39
Shrimp Boil, 95

Cornish Hens
Cornish Hens with
  Stuffing, 108
Glazed Cornish Hens, 30
Grilled Cornish Hens, 83

Desserts. *See also* Cakes; Candy;
  Cookies; Cookies, Bar;
  Ice Cream; Pies
Apples and Crumbles, 53
Banana Boats, 35
Bananas Faster, 53
Brown Bear in an
  Orchard, 33
Camp Peach Cobbler, 54
Caramel Fondue, 103
Cheesecake, 101
Cheese Flan, 94
Dirt Cake, 101
Dutch Oven Cobbler, 31
Fruit Dumplings, 53
Fruit Pizza, 96
Hawaiian Delights, 29
Melon Compote, 96
Mock Angel Food Cake, 33
No-Bake Fruitcake, 108
Nutty Apple Crisp, 57
Peach Cobbler, 65
Peach Delight, 53
Picnic Chocolate Fondue, 32
Pie Iron Dessert, 54
Pineapple Cheesecake, 97
Strawberry Delight, 103
Tropical Sundaes, 96
Victory Dessert Pizza, 21

Dips
Citrus Dip, 19
Dill Dip, 8
Dried Beef Dip, 101
Favorite Guacamole, 92
Hawaiian Cheese Dip, 94
Mexican Platter Dip, 92
Piña Colada Fruit Dip, 66
Queso, 60
Sausage and Cheese Dip, 58
Spinach Dip in Bread Bowl, 14
Yummy Fruit Dip, 15

Egg Dishes
Bacon and Egg Burritos, 28
Breakfast in a Bag, 48
California Egg Crackle, 48
Cowboy's Breakfast, 49
Creole Scramble, 28
Eggs in Bologna, 48
Milk Carton Eggs, 49
Rice Scramble, 28
Scrambled Egg Casserole, 17
Shipwreck Breakfast, 48

Fish. *See also* Salmon
"Batchelor" Flounder, 46
Broiled Grouper Steaks, 46
Foil-Baked Fish, 47
Foiled Fish, 46
Fried Fish Fillets, 106
Gingery Swordfish Steaks, 86
Grilled Catfish, 84
Grilled Cod with Dill, 84
Grilled Shark Steak, 85
Grilled Snapper with
  Lemon, 85
Grilled Swordfish, 86
Halibut in Foil, 85
Hot Creamy Tunaburgers, 47
Hot Tunawiches, 47
Montana Fish Fry, 47
Provençal Sea Bass, 46
Redfish with Dijon Sauce, 84
Smoked Trout, 87
Smokey Catfish, 84
Surprise Seafood Packets, 48
Sweet-and-Sour Swordfish, 86
Tangy Grilled Fish, 86
Tuna Mold Appetizer, 56

Index

Frankfurters
Bacon-Wrapped Dogs, 41
Beany Weeny, 42
Cheese Dog, 42
Chili Dogs in a Blanket, 42
Firecracker Franks, 98
Frank Kabobs, 42
Frankwiches, 42
Potatoes and Franks, 33
Potted Franks, 22
Sweet-and-Sour
Franks, 95

Frostings
Cream Cheese Frosting, 114

Ground Beef
Barbecued Beans, 64
Bean Casserole, 49
Beefy Noodles, 37
Brunswick Chili, 63
Calico Beans, 26
Campfire Lasagna, 38
Corny Stew, 39
Devil's Delight Chili, 37
Dutch Oven Stew, 39
Everyday Drumsticks, 75
Fannie Sue's Meat
Loaf, 112
Fruity Burger Filling, 16
Green Pepper
Burgers, 39
Ground Beef Bundles, 38
Gumboburgers, 39
Hobo Burgers, 75
Hobo Dinner, 38
Ho-Bo Dinners, 37
Hobo Hamburger, 33
Iron Skillet Casserole, 93
Meat Loaf Swirl, 23
Oriental Burgers, 75
Party-Perfect Pizza, 75
Pie Iron Pizza, 38
Pizza Loaves, 39
Prickly Meatballs, 38
Queso, 60
Spiced Patties, 99
Stuffinburgers, 58
Three-Bean Bake, 49
Torpedo Burger, 59

Ham
Cola Ham, 40
Ham-Cabbage Bundles, 40
Ham Knapsacks, 40
Hobo Meal, 43

Ice Cream
Banana Frozen Yogurt, 67
Candy Cane Ice Cream, 109
Country-Style Ice Cream, 97
Lemon Velvet Ice Cream, 97
Peanut Butter Ice Cream, 97

Kabobs
Beef Kabobs, 72
Cheesy Bread Kabobs, 106
Chicken Kabobs, 81
Chicken Liver Kabobs, 81
Chicken Yogurt Kabobs, 81
Famous Shish Kabobs, 73
Fiesta Beef Kabobs, 73
Frank Kabobs, 42
Fruit Kabobs, 19
Ground Lamb Kabobs, 76
Korean Sirloin Skewers, 72
Marinated Kabobs, 72
Marinated Skewered Lamb, 76
Mexican Kabobs, 73
Peanut Chicken Skewers, 83
Sausage-Chicken Kabobs, 102
Shrimp and Chicken Kabobs, 88
Shrimp and Scallop Kabobs, 88
Sirloin Kabobs, 74
Steak Strips en Brochette, 74
Sweet-Sour Lamb Skewers, 20
Teriyaki Kabobs, 74
Teriyaki Pinwheels, 67

Lamb
Barbecued Butterflied Lamb, 76
Barbecued Lamb, 76
Barbecued Rack of Lamb, 76
Ground Lamb Kabobs, 76
Marinated Skewered Lamb, 76
Sweet-Sour Lamb Skewers, 20

Marinades
Club Marinade, 90
Jane's Grilling Marinade, 90
Teriyaki Marinade, 90

Masterful One-Pot Meals, 120

Menus
A Potless-Luck Supper, 34
Backpacker's Lunch, 32
Backyard Luau, 94
Backyard Potluck Dinner, 62
Balcony Barbecue, 60
Banquet on Wheels, 8
Burger Bonanza, 58
Campfire Breakfast, 28
Citrus Bowl Tailgate, 19
Dutch Oven Dinner, 30
Great Expectations Graduation
    Party, 92
Grilled Garden Supper, 65
Hobo Feast, 33
Lighten Up Barbecue, 66
Oktoberfest Tailgate
    Party, 22
Old-Fashioned Ice Cream
    Cranking, 97
Outdoor Wedding
    Reception, 104
Picnic in a Pail, 10
Picnic in the Park, 15
Playhouse Warming, 109
Red, White and Blue Bash, 98
Road Rally Picnic, 11
Seaside Buffet, 105
Special Holiday Dinner, 107
Steeplechase Picnic, 13
Tailgate Barbecue, 24
Tailgate Brunch, 17
TGIF Pool Party, 101
Weekend Brunch, 56
Whitewater Canoeing
    Feast, 29

Muffins
Chocolate Chip Muffins, 21
Lemon Raspberry
    Muffins, 18
Muffins in Orange Cups, 29
Muffins in Orange Shells, 52
Peabody Muffins, 18

Pancakes
Peanut Pancakes, 52
Yeast Pancakes, 52

Pasta
Beefy Noodles, 37
Campfire Lasagna, 38
Chicken Spaghetti, 111

Pies
Chocolate Almond Pie, 61
Chocolate Chess Pies, 26
Egg Custard Pie, 114
Lemonade Pies, 64

Pizza
Fruit Pizza, 96
Party-Perfect Pizza, 75
Pie Iron Pizza, 38
Pizza Cheese Wheels, 12
Pizza Loaves, 39
Victory Dessert Pizza, 21

Pork
Bacon and Egg Burritos, 28
Bacon-Wrapped Cabbage, 50
Beany Weeny, 42
Beef and Bacon Twirls, 56
Best-Ever Pork Chops, 77
Breakfast in a Bag, 48
California Egg Crackle, 48
Country Short Ribs, 41
Cowboy's Breakfast, 49
Devil's Delight Chili, 37
Fabulous Ribs, 78
German Pork Chops, 41
Grilled Country-Style
    Ribs, 78
Grilled Marinated Pork, 77
Grilled Rice Casserole, 103
Hobo Meal, 43
Lone Star Ribs, 78
Marinated Pork Chops, 77
Peppery Barbecued Ribs, 65
Pigs in Mufflers, 11
Pork Bundles, 40
Pork Chops Plus, 30
Queso, 60
Sausage and Cheese Dip, 58
Sausage Balls, 17
Sausage-Chicken Kabobs, 102
Sausage Stew, 41
Shipwreck Breakfast, 48
Sorghum Main Dish Beans, 100

Index

Index

Super Skillet Supper, 43
Supreme Pâté, 107
Tailgate Barbecue, 25
Teriyaki Pork Chops, 77

Potatoes. *See also* Salads, Potato
Campfire French Fries, 50
Country Potatoes, 112
Creamy Potato Bake, 106
Dashed Potatoes, 67
Dutch Oven Potatoes, 51
Grilled Potatoes, 35
Grilled Potato Wedges, 50
Onioned Potatoes, 61
Potato Casserole, 112
Potatoes and Franks, 33
Shrimp Boil, 95
Sour Cream Potatoes, 59, 64
Spudnuts, 113
Super Skillet Supper, 43

Poultry. *See* Chicken; Cornish Hens;
Turkey

Salads, Fruit
Easy Fruit Salad, 17
Hot Knapsack Salad, 34
Old-Fashioned Fruit Salad, 62
Trail Salad, 32

Salads, Gelatin
Blueberry Salad, 99
Congealed Vegetable Salad, 63
Strawberry Pretzel Salad, 99

Salads, Main Dish
Patio Tuna Salad, 110
Seafood Pasta Salad, 8

Salads, Pasta
Golden Pasta Salad, 111
Macaroni Ring Salad, 61
Patio Tuna Salad, 110
Seafood Pasta Salad, 8
Yummy Mac Salad, 56

Salads, Potato
Baked Potato Salad, 26
German Potato Salad, 23
Make-Ahead Potato Salad, 100

Salads, Vegetable
Broccoli-Cauliflower Salad, 58
Broccoli Salad, 111
Campers' Salad, 30
Congealed Vegetable Salad, 63
Crunchy Vegetable Salad, 63
Cucumber-Onion Salad, 13
Lettuce Salad, 102
Low-Cal Vegetable Salad, 66
Marinated Veggies, 60
Parsley-Bulgur Salad, 15
Romaine-Tangerine Salad, 19
Sauerkraut Salad, 22
Spinach Salad, 107
Tail Light Tomatoes, 12
Vegetable Marinade Supreme, 105

Salmon
Barbecued Salmon, 47
Fresh Salmon, 85
Salmon-Zucchini Bundles, 34
Teriyaki Salmon Steaks, 85

Sandwiches
Bananawiches, 10
Beach Steak Sandwich, 37
Gumboburgers, 39
Ham Knapsacks, 40
Hiker's Treats, 32
Hobo Burgers, 75
Hot Creamy Tunaburgers, 47
Hot Tunawiches, 47
Oriental Burgers, 75
Oriental Chicken Pitas, 20
Pita Twins, 16
Roll-Up Sandwiches, 109
Spamwiches, 40
Studeabaked Sub, 12
Stuffinburgers, 58
Tea Sandwiches, 104
Torpedo Burger, 59

Sauces
Barbecue Sauce, 89
Barbecue Sauce for 100, 89
Easy Barbecue Sauce, 90
Flip 'em Dip 'em Sauce, 90
Mr. David's Barbecue Sauce, 89
Peppery Barbecue Sauce, 89
Snappy Sauce, 90

Spicy Barbecue Sauce, 88
Sweet Barbecue Sauce, 88
White Barbecue Sauce, 89

Seafood. *See also* Fish; Salmon;
      Shrimp
Barbecued Prawns, 105
Seafood Pasta Salad, 8
Secret Crab Spread, 62
Shrimp and Scallop Kabobs, 88
Surprise Seafood Packets, 48

Shrimp
Lime Marinated Shrimp, 87
Pool Party Shrimp, 102
Ragin' Cajun Shrimp, 87
Shrimp and Chicken Kabobs, 88
Shrimp and Scallop Kabobs, 88
Shrimp Boil, 95

Side Dishes
Garlic Cheese Grits, 18
Grilled Rice Casserole, 103
Slow-Cooker Apples, 18
Wild Rice, 113

Snacks
Apple Slices, 32
Apple Snackers, 10
Goody Cones, 11
Knots on a Log, 10
Shaggy Dogs, 54
S'Mores and More, 32

Spreads
Chili Cheese Ball, 24
Christmas Cheese Ball, 107

Homemade Pimento Cheese, 110
Old-Fashioned Cheese Ball, 62
Secret Crab Spread, 62
Tuna Mold Appetizer, 56
Two-Cheese Ball, 105

Stews. *See also* Chili
Campfire Stew, 36
Corny Stew, 39
Dutch Oven Beef Stew, 36
Dutch Oven Stew, 39
Sausage Stew, 41

Tomatoes
Tail Light Tomatoes, 12

Turkey
Fried Wild Turkey, 83
Grilled Turkey Burgers, 58
Turkey Caribe, 83
Turkey Sausage Filling, 16

Vegetables. *See also* Beans;
      Coleslaw; Corn; Potatoes;
      Salads, Potato; Salads,
      Vegetable; Tomatoes
Bacon-Wrapped Cabbage, 50
Cabbage Casserole, 112
Foil-Baked Onions, 50
Grilled Fresh Vegetables, 51
Grilled Onions, 103
Marinated Copper Carrots, 65
Vegetable Medley, 31
Zucchini Parmesan, 51

Venison
Smoked Venison, 78

Index

Published by Favorite Recipes® Press
an imprint of

2451 Atrium Way
Nashville, Tennessee 37214
1-800-358-0560